50 dates in 50 states

"I could not put down this book once I had begun to read. Why? Because it's compelling reading—as well as sharing her own remarkable story, each chapter gave me insights about my own life and work. I often say that our greatest strength is our fallibility—Melanie proves this in her open and honest portrayal of life and work and lets you into her secrets of success.

Melanie is a wise practitioner, we can all learn from her book. I will keep this book close—like a best friend for life."

—Dr. Andrew Machon, London, United Kingdom
International Executive, Business Coach and Author

"Melanie Brocklehurst is an exceptional executive and has now proved herself to be an exceptional author and coach. *50 Dates in 50 States: One Woman's Journey to Positive Change* provides a practical guide for those wanting to make positive changes as Melanie openly shares her 8-step Positive Change Formula wrapped wonderfully in the story of the past year of her life. You are going to love both the book and the positive changes that you achieve through putting her formula into practice!"

—Bonnie Boezeman AO, Sydney, Australia
Managing Director, Business Benefits International

"What's better than a dating guide? Answer: A book that helps you with dating, provides you with a formula to achieve positive change and is wrapped up in a story! Melanie has created a unique and exciting book that is part travelogue, part romp and part how-to coach yourself happy. In her book, 50 Dates in 50 States, Melanie doesn't patronize you. She, like me, shows that to find the right life partner isn't necessarily 'easy' or 'simple' but that the results are worth it."

—Marla Martenson, Los Angeles, United States
Author of Excuse Me, Your Soul Mate is Waiting

50 dates in 50 states

One Woman's Journey to POSITIVE CHANGE

M.L.BROCKLEHURST

NEW YORK

50 dates in 50 states
One Woman's Journey to POSITIVE CHANGE

ISBN 978-1-61448-637-4 paperback
ISBN 978-1-61448-638-1 eBook
ISBN 978-1-61448-639-8 audio
Library of Congress Control Number: 2013933175

Morgan James Publishing
The Entrepreneurial Publisher
5 Penn Plaza, 23rd Floor
New York City, New York 10001
(212) 655-5470 office • (516) 908-4496 fax
www.MorganJamesPublishing.com

Cover Design by:
Rachel Lopez
www.r2cdesign.com

Interior Design by:
Bonnie Bushman
bonnie@caboodlegraphics.com

In an effort to support local communities, raise awareness and funds, Morgan James Publishing donates a percentage of all book sales for the life of each book to Habitat for Humanity Peninsula and Greater Williamsburg.

Get involved today, visit
www.MorganJamesBuilds.com.

In Memory Of

Adam Hays

Adamski
You will always live on in my heart.
You are my soul mate and my inspiration.
I will never forget you and I will never stop
loving you.

Life is either a daring adventure or nothing. Security does not exist in nature, nor do the children of men as a whole experience it. Avoiding danger is no safer in the long run than exposure.

—**Helen Keller**

Table of Contents

	FOREWORD	XIII
	INTRODUCTION	XV
Chapter 1	PROBLEMS	1
Chapter 2	THE POSITIVE CHANGE FORMULA	13
Chapter 3	OPTIONS	17
Chapter 4	SOLUTIONS	19
Chapter 5	IMPLEMENTATION	27
	The Best Laid Plans...	33
	The Start of the 50 Dates	
	California	36
	Date #1: Chris – Life Is A Rollercoaster	*38*
	Date #2: Sam – Making Out At The Drive-In	*41*
	Arizona	48
	Date #3: Diego – Allergies And Rock Concerts	*49*
	New Mexico, Texas, Oklahoma, Arkansas	57
	Date #4: Nathan – Scary Stalker Material	*57*

Dates #5&6: Dylan & Tom – Vegetarians And Memorials　59

Date #7: Josh – Another Ex-Girlfriend On The List?　60

Tennessee　62

Date #8: Steven – You Missed Out On
Some Great Hickory-Smoked Ribs!　66

Mississippi　67

Date #9: Richard – I Need A Coke Hit!　68

Chapter 6　TENACITY　71

Louisiana　72

Date #10: Max – Music And Magic In New Orleans　73

Alabama　79

Date #11: Adrian - Safety First　79

Florida　83

Date #12: Mark – Three's A Crowd,
Leave Your Smart Phone At Home　83

Georgia　87

Date #13: Phil – Art And Truck-Driving　87

Chapter 7　INTEGRITY　91

California, again... and Nevada!　92

Date #14: Sam – The Official Date in Las Vegas　97

A Military Operation　101

Maryland　103

Date #15: Andrew – Jumping Straight Back On The Horse　104

Washington D.C.　105

Date #16: Luke – A Walk In The Park　106

Virginia, North Carolina, South Carolina, New York,
Pennsylvania, New Jersey and Delaware　107

Dates #17 – 23: Too Many To Mention　107

Wisconsin, Indiana, Michigan　109

Date #26: Jacob – Moonwalking in Gary, Indiana　111

Illinois　113

Date #27: Roger – The Job Interview　113

Minnesota, North Dakota, Idaho, Utah　117

Date #28: Roberto – The Restorer Of Faith　119

Omaha, Iowa, South Dakota, Montana,
Wyoming, West Virginia, Ohio, Kentucky,
Missouri, Kansas and Colorado... Phew!   121
 Dates #34-36: Toby – Banter And Bickering
  In The Badlands   *121*
Hawaii   127
 Date #43: Jonny – Swimming With The Sharks   *128*
Mexico   130
 Date #44: José – My Unofficial Date   *136*
Back in the UK with my family   141

Chapter 8 VICTORY   146
 Mexico again... and 8 of the 9 states   146
 New Hampshire, Vermont, Maine, Massachusetts,
 Rhode Island, Connecticut, Oregon, Washington   148
  Dates #45-50: Charlie – Charlie And
  The Hot Chocolate Factories of New England   *148*
  Dates #51&52: Harry And Ian – I Left My Heart In... *149*
 Alaska   154
  Date #53: José – My Last Official Date   *154*

Chapter 9 EVALUATION...   156
 The Final Stage of the Positive Change Formula   156
 Life after 50 Dates   157

Chapter 10 THE POSITIVE CHANGE FORMULA IN
 ACTION ALL OVER AGAIN   160
 Kick-Start the Positive   162

EPILOGUE   167

AFTERWORD   169

ABOUT THE AUTHOR   171

POSITIVE CHANGE COACHING AND CONSULTING   173

ACKNOWLEDGEMENTS   175

Foreword

When Melanie walked into my *Three Days to Cash* workshop in San Diego in August 2011, I could tell by her energy that she had the passion and drive to succeed.

After hearing why she was in the US, I loved her idea of completing 50 dates in 50 states and admired her commitment to finding love – something we all strive for.

What I couldn't believe was she hadn't seen what an amazing story it would make and I persuaded her there and then to put pen to paper. She had to sell something at the workshop so I urged her to sell the book and, not surprisingly, she made the most sales at the event.

It can be a lonely time at the beginning of any journey and I was pleased that Melanie found new friends and support in the *Live Out Loud* community.

Throughout her journey I have been privileged to watch Melanie grow and inspire others with her story. She has a great ability to capture an audience and create a belief in those around her that they, too, can achieve their dreams.

Melanie knows and understands the pressures of life and talks candidly about these experiences in her book. Her positive attitude shines through when she notes that the best thing about hitting rock bottom is knowing that afterwards, the only way is up!

In this book, Melanie not only talks about her dates but also discusses openly the secret to her many life successes—past and present. She provides a clear and simple equation through her Positive Change Formula that allows anyone to achieve the positive results they want in life, no matter what the obstacles.

After this remarkable life journey, I am not surprised that Melanie has become a professional coach and is working with people to inspire, rally and support them in identifying and implementing their goals and desires. Even at my workshop it was clear that it is her nature to provide assistance to people who are struggling, feeling alone or just needing that extra push to get ahead.

In this book, Melanie provides you with a wonderful gift: the tools you need to get ahead and achieve all of those positive changes you want in life. As a bonus she does this through an inspiring and funny story.

So, find yourself a comfortable spot. Read slowly. Enjoy each step of the formula as the story unfolds, happy in the knowledge that after reading this book you too will be equipped to achieve your dreams!

—**Loral Langemeier**, Zephyr Cove, Nevada
Bestselling author of *The Millionaire Maker*

Introduction

On the 23rd of June 2008 I lost my soul mate, Adam. He was thirty-seven. There was a lesson in his death but I wasn't ready to learn it until 2011, when I literally hit rock bottom, falling down the stairs and collapsing in the front room of my house with exhaustion.

As a goal-driven, career-focused, workaholic who loved to travel, I should have been living my dream. Heading up the Government Relations section for an international corporation in Sydney, Australia, I travelled abroad every month and worked in a dynamic, fast-paced environment. It was what I'd been working towards since starting my career.

I'd also been offered a great opportunity at Head Office in the US and to my friends, colleagues and the outside world it appeared that my life was on the up.

My work had provided me with great solace in the past. It was the one thing I felt I could really control and it had given me a safe place to hide since Adam's death.

However, for several months, I'd been struggling to hold things together. I hadn't taken a weekend off in more than two years and, although I'd hoped keeping busy would help me eventually get over my grief, it had really only postponed the inevitable.

At the start of 2011, that grief finally caught up with me and consumed me totally. I could no longer bury it with work. I felt completely void inside; the only feelings I had were emptiness and pain.

The fact that I was still able to function at a high level in a difficult job and hide my inner turmoil was no longer serving me. I felt incredibly lonely and wondered if anyone actually cared enough to see the real me.

All of the tools I'd used in the past to survive and thrive were creating the opposite effect, and that scared the hell out of me. I felt as though my world was turning upside down and inside out, and no one could help.

Unbeknown to even my best friend, on a nightly basis, I had to talk myself out of downing pills and permanently ending my pain.

It took me hitting this rock bottom to finally find the courage to break out of the shackles I'd wrapped myself in.

Eventually, with effort and support, I pulled myself out of the depths and began to discover what truly makes me happy. I identified the positive changes I wanted to make and moved from feeling disconnected to everyone to now being reconnected with my family and friends.

This book is about that journey to wholeness. Along the way I quit my job, sold my house, travelled around the US having fifty dates in fifty states, and eventually met the man who loves me and accepts me as I am.

I also discovered a desire to help others make positive changes too. As I spoke to people before, during, and after my trip, I was amazed and saddened by how many had dreams they were leaving unfulfilled. Many told me they thought that what I was doing was incredibly brave and they would like to have the courage to do something similar in their lives too.

It struck me that no matter how me, me, me, the media portrays society, in fact most people are not living for themselves. This is hardly surprising given that, from an early age, we're taught to conform and compromise. And while I'm not espousing anarchy, I've found through this year's experience that when I'm truly living the life I want to live, the people around me are equally given permission to live their dreams— and we are all happier.

It's my hope that my story will inspire people to follow a process I named the Positive Change Formula and achieve their dreams before they get to the point I reached. I understand how difficult it is to break free but I know if I can do it—anyone can!

CHAPTER 1

Problems

I've never understood people who, to coin a good English phrase, are 'All mouth, no trousers', which means they talk a lot but never act, or, bitch a lot but never do anything to improve the situation.

I've always been a person of action—in fact occasionally I need to think a bit more before I jump in! I'm also a person who keeps my issues to myself. I generally manage to maintain a happy facade to my work colleagues, friends and even my family, with the exception of my best mate, Georgia.

Miss G, as I call her, knows pretty much everything because we spend so much time together. She was my surrogate husband until I found the poor bugger who was foolish enough to fall in love with me!

I've often joked she'd make a wonderful partner as she's a great cook, independent, a good conversationalist and we have a lot of common interests. She's also a dark-haired, clear-skinned amazon who stands six feet tall with no shoes on. In fact, the only reason we're not a match made in heaven is she is a she and so am I, and neither of us are that way inclined.

However, even Miss G had no idea of the depth of my depression and despair at the beginning of 2011, or that I was having a daily conversation to stop myself from downing pills in my house. Even with her I couldn't share how far I'd sunk.

I felt that I was becoming one of those 'all mouth, no trousers' people, even though the chatter was only in my head. I felt literally and physically stuck, which for such an action-oriented person was a very unfamiliar feeling.

Since I was a kid I've been good at compartmentalising and that ability got me through the past couple of years since Adam's death. It was how I handled, or, perhaps, mishandled, my grief. It is an innate part of me that is hard to turn off at will. However, for whatever reason, I seemed to have lost that ability.

It is a scary thing to suddenly lose a skill you have been reliant upon your whole life. To be honest, until I lost it, I never even considered it as a skill. It just was.

Then it was gone and I was left to contemplate life without it as well as without Adam. Life without Adam was one thing I couldn't stop thinking about, no matter how hard I worked and tried to cram my brain with other things. That thought—life without Adam—kept permeating every waking moment.

You would think that after almost three years, the fact that I would never see or talk to Adam again would have sunk in, but such is the power of compartmentalising. I had managed not to face the reality of the situation until it hit all at once.

I started dating Adam, who was a family friend from way back, when I was nineteen. I'd had a crush on him since I was a young spotty teenager and I couldn't believe my luck when we got together.

Adam always reminded me of a Native American, with his strong nose, olive skin and long, dark hair that flowed to the middle of his back. His resemblance to the Native American was further reinforced with his deep love of nature and of being in the woods. He had a sharp brain but a philosopher's heart and chose to follow his own path and worked where he was happiest—outside. He was exotic and totally different from me.

Although we were both by nature recreationally inclined, enjoying weekends and holidays far more than work, Adam indulged this side of his nature to a far greater extent than I did. He saw the trap of the nine to five work life and vowed not to fall into it. Whereas, I believed it was the only way there was and worked hard to get ahead of the other worker bees.

I trusted him as much as I'd trusted anyone but, to my great disappointment, he betrayed that trust on a night out in London with some girl he met at a club.

Two years after we got together, after I had just turned twenty-one, we went our separate ways. More upset than I was willing to show, I escaped the situation by planning and disappearing on a year-long trip around the world. I travelled for months around Africa and then on to Australia, New Zealand, Asia and America.

In Australia I met and fell in love with the man I eventually married, but despite that, I never stopped loving Adam.

Adam left the UK a year after I did to do his own travelling, and neither of us had really gone back for any longer than a short visit. I settled in Australia with my husband, and Adam didn't settle anywhere but spent a long time roaming India, Nepal, Thailand and other parts of Asia.

We had caught up with each other in person almost immediately after my marriage finding that we were in Sydney, Australia at the same time. Sat on the bed of my hotel room I shared with him the photos of my wedding and the sad reality that things had irrevocably changed settled on both of us.

Shortly after, Adam left Australia. Over the next five years we stayed in touch mainly via phone and email, each having an uncanny ability to know when to reach out during the times one of us was in some sort of life crisis.

He knew of my divorce after only a few short years of marriage and of my travels and the steps I was taking up the career ladder. I knew of his escapades working at various times teaching English, helping in the hospitals in Calcutta or as an extra in an Indian Bollywood movie.

And eventually, he returned to Australia in 2006. He stayed with me for many weeks during which time we had some intense conversations about the possibility of getting back together.

However, newly single and having survived an intense and passionate but emotionally debilitating relationship, I was not ready and told Adam so. He left again after a bitter argument.

But, as always, I felt a pull to reconnect. We had acknowledged years before that we were soul mates, despite not seeming to be able to make it work in a relationship. So, after I had taken some time to heal from the emotional wreckage of my last relationship, I again reached out to him. It was now 2007.

I knew after leaving me he had been winding his way back to the UK and after several months of not getting a reply to my emails, which was not like Adam, I rang his parents' house.

I was shocked to find he was still in the country—Adam was not one to stay put for any length of time. However, the reason why he was there was still more shocking.

I was totally floored as he explained why he was speaking more slowly and deliberately than usual. He told me over the phone that he'd had a stroke. It turned out he had a heart problem he'd unknowingly lived with since birth.

I wanted to get straight on a plane there and then but Adam calmly reassured me that everything would be fine. He was scheduled for a heart operation that he said was as routine as those kinds of things can be— and he was a lot younger and fitter than most people who underwent the surgery—so he was confident there would be no problems.

Despite me wanting to cancel the trek to Nepal I had already booked—having been inspired by Adam's descriptions of the country the year before—Adam insisted I go, eager for me to experience it. We spoke regularly in the lead up to the trek and in the aftermath. And whilst I was in Nepal, Adam underwent his first heart operation.

Now at the start of 2008, Adam successfully pulled through his first operation but needed a second. As I worked in Parliament House providing legal and policy advice to the Minister for Home Affairs, Adam worked hard to regain some of the skills he had lost during his stroke and to cope with life's daily activities.

I knew he was having difficulty concentrating and reading so I sent him an occasional audio book of our favourite author, Terry Pratchett, and asked him to do some research on the internet of trips to countries we both still wanted to visit.

We started to make tentative travel plans and although Adam occasionally hinted he may not be able to head overseas for a while, we indulged our passion together and talked of holidays we could take to Oman, Qatar and other exotic places.

We also talked of his other passion, his son. For various reasons Adam had not seen him for a long time but he still thought of him every day and the pain of not being in contact was evident as he spoke. He planned to reconnect with him in a few years when he turned eighteen and hoped to finally share with him all the things he'd been holding inside.

The intimacy between Adam and I deepened and we began to end each call with, 'I love you'.

Unbeknown to Adam I booked myself on a flight back to the UK in late July. After Nepal I had needed to save some more vacation time but I was determined to surprise him during Federal Parliament's winter recess.

I was literally weeks away from seeing Adam again and being able to hug and kiss him, when he died.

Everyone who knew him believed totally that he would be fine as he was young, strong and vibrant. But, despite surviving his second heart operation, a few days later he was no longer with us. It was the 23rd of June 2008.

I was standing in my kitchen when the call came. When I heard the news I couldn't breathe and couldn't respond. I found myself gasping for air and simply repeating one word, 'No. No. No.'

I put the phone down and retreated to the bedroom where I sobbed uncontrollably. My brain clouded over as I refused to take in the news.

The next day when I went to work even the Minister stopped when he saw me, aghast at the state I was in. My usually bouncy red hair was lank, my eyes red raw and my face puffy from all of the crying and lack of sleep.

I still couldn't say what had happened, it hurt too much, but he told me if I had to get on a plane I should do so and not worry about Parliament and the next few sitting weeks. By the end of the workday I'd changed the flights I'd booked back to England and was leaving less than twenty-four hours later.

I flew back still in disbelief. I sat with his parents as they organised his funeral and we talked fondly of the past and the times I'd spent with all of them. At that stage I think none of us could really believe what was happening. I wanted to see Adam's body to make it real for me but was unable to as there was no viewing and the casket was kept closed.

So, I went to the funeral with some of our mutual friends who hadn't even known Adam was sick and were doubly shocked by the news. I stood at the back trying to take in what was going on. I remember a friend holding me up as I teetered slightly because my body temperature kept swinging between hot to cold as I fought to keep control of my emotions.

I was filled with remorse and regret, and still am, that I didn't get back in time nor tell Adam I was coming. Perhaps he would have held on.

As my coping mechanism, I turned to my faithful old friend, work, to keep me busy and my head occupied so I didn't have to deal with the grief. I moved from the Minister's office, where people knew vaguely what had happened, to a new high-flying corporate job where no one knew me or my past.

In that environment I thought I could more easily hide my shame and bury my regret at not being there for Adam. I thought I could forget the pain and disappointment of not being able to tell him I loved him in person and of our never getting to fulfil our travel plans.

And then, over three years, I worked myself to the point of a nervous breakdown.

Apart from getting sick all the time with minor ailments that everyone attributed to being a side effect of my working so hard, rather than as a symptom of my depression, I remained to the outside world a person who was functioning at a high level of competence in a difficult job.

No one saw the pain beneath the veil, which led me to believe no one cared. Put simply, I was spiralling down in a vicious circle. More often than not, the only way I could see to get any peace was to commit suicide. And with Adam's death this had the extra appeal of being reunited with him.

I did cry and grieve a little just after he died and even went for some grief counselling, but then I shut that grief out.

I also gradually shut out everyone else in my life by keeping them, as well as myself, in the dark about just how hurt, angry, distraught, empty, guilty and a whole host of other powerfully negative emotions I was holding inside.

After almost three years, I guess the strain became too much, and all of those feelings engulfed me. I was no longer compartmentalising. I was hiding.

Then the day of awakening came.

In late March 2011, I fell down the stairs and collapsed in the front room of my house. I lay on the floor for an hour, wracked with tears and pain and feeling that I had literally hit rock bottom.

For the entire time my iPod was playing in the kitchen but I had been virtually unaware of it until Andrew Lloyd Webber's *All I Ask of You* started playing and the words began to filter into my consciousness.

Along with the words, I heard my inner voice urging me to listen. The lyrics connected with my heart and resonated with my soul. My inner voice was echoing the sentiments: No more talk of darkness. I am here. I will look after you. I have always been here guiding you.

When I was younger my inner voice would talk to me a lot. It was a quiet, calming voice that had always proved to reassure me and guide me in difficult circumstances. I hadn't heard it for years but it was there with me at the bottom of the stairs like a wise, kindly grandparent, seeking to calm me and arrest my tears.

I gradually stopped sobbing and listened to the rest of the song. By the end I was breathing deeply and feeling perfectly calm. I realised I wasn't alone and I knew that the answers to creating the life I wanted were inside of me—I just needed to find them and trust myself again.

I suddenly felt that I could see everything more clearly. What was important and what was not. And I found my life sadly lacking. Yes, I had a great career and a good friend but where were the rest of my friends? Where was my family? And where was the love in my life?

Over the next few weeks, I examined my life and my choices.

I realised that because I had gradually shut myself off from feeling true love and intimacy with others, I had removed any vitality I had for life.

Along with that vitality, despite my long hours at work, I'd lost my focus, energy and drive. An intensely scary thought, as, maintaining a focus on the future had always inspired me to get through whatever shit was happening in the present.

For the past two years, I'd been working in a US-owned global corporation in Australia, and, despite having a great job offer and potential relocation to America, I realised that the thought of starting again and having to play the facade of happy Mel, intelligent Mel, career-focussed and driven Mel to a whole host of new people just filled me with dread. But if that wasn't in my future, what was?

I considered my skills: law, policy, political knowledge could be transferred to another job. Research, oral, written communication, negotiation skills etc were still intact despite my lack of interest and waning concentration levels.

However, I was beginning to doubt all of my innate gifts. My intuition. My ability to read people and anticipate danger: two vital skills that had not surprisingly helped greatly in my profession as a lawyer, political adviser and lobbyist. All of these, I was beginning to question and wonder whether in fact the issues I was now seeing were nothing more than paranoia.

Now questioning all of the innate gifts I had previously taken for granted, I considered what I had left and realised what it was: Resilience.

As I looked back over a childhood that was marked with intensely unhappy times, I could see that there were also times of peace brought about by my resilience. It led me to escape to the dream world of books, it led me to my love of horses which provided a reason to leave the house and enjoy the happiness and freedom of galloping across the Derbyshire moors. And it led me to study hard, which provided me with the tools to escape.

Despite my wariness and distrust of those people in my life who were closest to me and whom I should have been able to rely on, my resilience remained intact.

I've no idea what it is within me that has always refused to be a victim and made me as resilient as I am, but to this day if you knock me down I'll get up fighting. My parents called it stubborn. I call it determined. Whatever it is, I'm grateful for possessing that spirit.

And as I examined where I was in my life I found that there was still a spark in me wanting to fight.

Perhaps, that spark was my inner voice, which had caused me to be in this phase of re-examination.

And, as clearly as I could now see that my resilience had remained intact, I could see that from an early age my ability to trust had been shattered.

Being pulled close and then pushed away is confusing but when the actions are scattered with unfulfilled promises they quickly lead to distrust. Learning not to rely on the words or actions of those closest to me, my lessons in not trusting others were reinforced at the age of sixteen, when I was date raped.

As I examined my many relationships since that event it was now clear that none of them really stood a chance. Although I had trusted Adam more than the rest, he had betrayed me too.

Consequently, when any of my later partners began to get close to me at a truly emotional level, my barriers came up and I started pushing them away.

I realised that in order to move forward I needed to do two important things. The first was to allow myself to grieve. The second was to finally make peace with my family and deal with my trust issues. I needed to own them as an adult.

In thinking about that time at sixteen after I had been date raped I realised I felt very similar now to how I had then. Empty. Frightened. Powerless. Feeling that I had no one to turn to. And yes, suicidal.

Back then I had attempted suicide. I was found lying in the stable with my best friend at the time, my horse, Figgie. Ghis and Phil, the couple who kept their horse next to mine, had begun to get worried when they hadn't seen me in the evening and leaned over the stable door to find Figgie nuzzling me as I laid next to the water buckets I had drunk from to help me swallow the tablets.

Luckily they acted quickly, talking to me and reminding me about all the fun times I had with them over the years they had known me, trying everything to keep me awake as they rushed me to hospital to have my stomach pumped.

When I left the hospital later that night I was angry and upset at still being alive. Not used to failing at something I put my mind to, I rationalised the situation and started to believe that the universe had a reason for keeping me around.

I had always felt I was on the earth for a reason. I just needed to work out what it was. My inner voice told me that I had not yet found it and from there I determined that I needed to continue to work hard and get away to university.

Twenty years later, having seriously considered suicide once again, I realised why I had not taken the pills this time. I had not lost the belief that I am here for a reason and I still haven't fulfilled my purpose. Until I did so, I could not leave this beautiful planet.

One night, as I contemplated these things, I had a compulsion to ring my dad. Like me, he isn't great when it comes to dealing with emotions but again, like me, he is good at problems that require reason and logic. When it comes to nutting out a complex issue (normally to do with work) I generally ring him for advice. On this occasion, I felt I needed to talk to him, so I picked up the phone and dialled, not even checking what time it was back in England.

He answered and I saw him in my mind, with his slightly shaggy silver hair and long pointy, lined face that had become rounder with age.

Since I'd left home he'd stopped trying to tell me what to do, knowing from experience that I rarely listened if I was directed to a specific course of action. Instead, he used his years of consulting and counselling business owners to ask me questions and lead me to the answers he wanted me to find.

'What's going on Meg?' he asked, using my family's nickname for me.

'Not much. Work. Crazy hours. No social life. The usual.' I replied sullenly.

'I've been telling you there's more to life than work. You know I regret missing all that time with you and Nic when you were growing up' he counselled.

'Yeah, well...' my voice trailed off.

'Come on, Meg! You've got a great job offer and move to the US to look forward to. You'll love it. And we can come and visit you more often. It will be great!' he said encouragingly, sounding like Churchill trying to rally the troops.

'Hmmm. I suppose so...'

'But...' he said and paused, obviously allowing me time to finish off the sentence.

'But, I don't get a good feeling about taking it,' I blurted out. 'I'm not enjoying my job here if I'm honest and I'm exhausted. If I go to the US I'm just going to work even harder as I always do when I start something new and I don't think I have the energy for that right now.'

'This is the first time you've said you're unhappy with your job,' he noted.

'Yeah. Well, I'm unhappy with a lot of things right now,' I replied mournfully.

There was a long pause before he asked, 'You remember the happiness scale we used when you were younger? On a scale of one to ten, how happy are you with your job right now?'

'A two or three.'

'And with your life?'

'The same.'

'How long has that been the case?'

'Around eighteen months.'

I heard him take a deep breath and then say, 'Sounds like it's time for a big change then, Meg. Don't you think?'

'Probably,' I agreed, placating him, although I still wasn't completely sure.

'OK, well I'll leave you to think about it. I've got to head to bowls.' (My dad is a crazy keen bowler.) 'I know you'll work it out.'

And with that I was left again to think.

Talking about the Happiness scale reminded me of something else that I'd used in my past and with anything I drag out of the recesses of my mind it came to me in a flash. My Positive Change Formula!

I'd created the formula after my attempted suicide whilst dreaming of the life I wanted to escape to and how to achieve it. I'd always loved travel and had decided even at age eight that I wanted to live in Australia and be a lawyer. I developed my formula as a way to keep focused and positive when that bright future I had long imagined was still years away.

I knew now it was time to drag out the formula, dust it off and apply it again to my life.

CHAPTER 2

The Positive
Change Formula

I had called the process I'd developed the Positive Change Formula because the eight steps in the equation spell the word POSITIVE.

The first step is to work out the **P**roblems I currently face.

The second is to brainstorm what **O**ptions there are to change the situation.

From that the third step is to identify the **S**olution, which leads to the next step of drafting an **I**mplementation plan.

Steps five and six are a little harder to quantify, requiring me to follow through with **T**enacity and **I**ntegrity.

Which result in the last two steps, the inevitable **V**ictory and a final **E**valuation of my new situation.

All of which spells POSITIVE. Simple!

I got up quickly and went in search of my big notepad. Tearing out sheets of paper I turned them so that instead of being longer lengthways they were longer in width (or in computer speak so that they were landscape rather than portrait). And then I wrote and circled one word in the middle of each: **P**roblems. **O**ptions. **S**olution. **I**mplementation. **T**enacity. **I**ntegrity. **V**ictory. **E**valuation.

From each of these words, I would create a mind-map.

I came across mind-mapping a few years ago. I can't remember how, but it has been amazing in helping me to clarify my thoughts.

From the circled word in the middle of each page I drew lines emanating outwards to link with new words that described thoughts, actions or ideas that related to the initial word in the middle. This created something that looked like a spider web as my thoughts jumped from one thing to another.

I started with the first step: **P**roblems.

Dad had unknowingly prompted me to identify a couple as I applied the happiness scale to my work and life in general.

So now, I applied it to other specific areas. I drew eight lines spiralling out from the word 'Problems' and wrote the following: romance; friends and family; health; spiritual; emotional; work; finances; and physical environment.

As I thought specifically about each of these areas I gave each a number on the happiness scale. Eeek! Mostly one to three was coming up in all areas – except financial which came out as an eight. Why?

I looked again at each of the eight areas I'd identified and drew further lines from each listing all the problems that I was facing in that specific area of my life.

For work it included exhaustion, lack of focus, lack of interest, a disconnection between the company's values and mine etc etc. There were a lot of links to the word 'work' and none of them were positive!

For health I wrote depression, tiredness, trouble concentrating, frequent stomach problems etc.

As I listed the issues in each area the same things kept cropping up: loneliness, disconnection, no time to relax, no time with friends, sick, unfit, exhausted.

I realised I was:

- Lonely. I missed Adam and having a soul mate or partner in my life.
- Disconnected. From my family and friends and importantly my values.
- Lacking in time to relax and time with those important to me.
- Sick, chubby and unfit.
- Disliking my job because I was exhausted.
- Living in the inner West of Sydney away from the hills, trees and countryside that I had always found so calming.
- Missing travelling.
- Bored stiff with the routine of my life.

Bloody hell! I looked at the list. Not allowing myself to grieve and drawing into myself had impacted every area of my life. Only my finances were doing well and even there I had a huge mortgage that scared me to think about. How had I let things get so bad?

The good news was, in identifying each of the key issues I had also identified the solutions or goals that I wanted to achieve. By flipping each problem, I saw what I wanted in life, which was to:

- Find a partner;
- Reconnect with my family and society in general;
- Spend time with my friends and have weekends off to relax;
- Regain my health and fitness;
- Change jobs to a career that feeds all of my intellectual parts, including my mind, body and spirit;
- Relocate to the countryside where I feel most at peace;
- Travel... a lot; and
- Break out of my routine, have some fun and adventures again.

I scanned the list, encouraged to see that they were all attainable goals. It wasn't as though I wanted to live on Mars.

I was now ready for the next step: Options. I retrieved the piece of paper which had this written in the middle of it.

'You're going to destroy a rainforest by the end of the day, Mel', I muttered to myself in a gleeful tone.

For the first time in the last couple of years I was excited.

CHAPTER 3

Options

L ooking at the word 'Options', I got to work on another mind-map. This time linked to the circled word I wrote down the goals that I wanted to achieve. And, branching out from each I started to brainstorm the options I had to achieve them.

So, for finding a partner, I could join an online dating site, go out to the pubs more, join a dance class, etc.

As for my job, the US was still an option, or I could find a new job in Australia, or quit and have a break for a while. There were other possibilities too, so I added those.

I was enjoying this exercise so much I ended up tearing out more paper as I had almost filled up one sheet just with identifying the options for two of the goals I'd set.

I needed more space but I didn't have any larger sheets! So, instead, I wrote down one of my identified goals in the middle of each new piece of paper and let my brain go wild thinking of all the ways I could achieve them.

After following the same process for each goal, I saw that the options generally ranged from doing nothing, tinkering around the edges, to drastic measures, which included selling the house and taking a year off to travel.

I noticed that simply in the act of thinking about and writing down different options I felt more alive with the possibilities and choices I had identified. The exercise itself had brought some of my energy back. I'd felt lethargic for so long because I'd lost all hope of having a good life but now in front of me were pages of options for achieving something better!

Armed with all of my new options, I went back to my linear way of thinking and wrote a pros and cons list for each.

For me going from expansive to detail works well because I know I'm considering the issue from every possible angle. It means the perfectionist in me is mollified.

Yes, I am a self-confessed anally retentive person who needs everything to be perfect. It means my house is always clean and I'm a good worker, but on the down side, I'm always disappointed as I can never get anything one hundred per cent right. Another issue to work on...

CHAPTER 4

Solutions

fter I'd drafted the pros and cons lists, I identified several variations of solutions and noticed that none felt quite right, although I was definitely leaning towards the drastic—selling up and travelling.

Travel had always been an important part of my life, expanding my view of the world and teaching me a lot of valuable lessons.

My last two big trips were to Nepal and had both had a very powerful impact on me. The first had reminded me just how lucky I was.

Trekking for five weeks in the freezing mountains with no mode of transport other than my feet, no means of washing other than with cold water from a small metal bowl and no place to sleep other than a tent (the inside of which would be covered in frost in the morning as my breathe and that of my friend, Annie, hit the lining and froze) was a great reminder of the daily luxuries I had been taking for granted.

It also opened my eyes to how fortunate I was as a female growing up in the West. I have always been a great advocate for equality and as a female I have never felt I was any less capable than my male counterparts. On the occasions I have felt I was being treated with less

19

respect than a male, I was armed with the education and skills to fight back and work to change this perception.

The girls in rural Nepal are not so lucky. Through talking to the locals in the mountains, I discovered that many girls do not receive any formal education at all, and an uneducated girl is of little value to her family making her parents susceptible to the fast talk of con men claiming to be from so-called 'employment agencies' in Kathmandu.

Whilst the families believe they are sending their daughters to undertake domestic work the sad truth is, according to the Australian Himalayan Foundation, almost as many as twenty thousand girls from the poorest parts of Nepal end up in Indian brothels or as slaves in other parts of the world.

It was this trip that caused me to realise the value of my education and the amazing choices and life it had provided me.

I remember speaking to Adam about it and finding a charity that specifically supported the girls through the provision of schools for them. Adam noticed when I spoke of the issue my voice raised and I got irate and animated discussing the issue.

'This really makes you angry doesn't it, Meg' he noted.

'I cannot help it but yes it does! Those girls are just as smart and deserving as their brothers and simply because they were born female they are being mistreated. It isn't fair and I cannot abide unfairness! I never tolerated it myself and cannot see why they should have to.' I blurted out speaking more from my heart than my head for a change.

'No need to apologise Meg, you are passionate about the plight of others less fortunate than you, it was one of the reasons why I loved you when we were together and why I always admired how hard you worked at University. If you want to do something to help those girls, I have no doubt you will.' Adam had said encouragingly.

The second trip to Nepal was taken after Adam's death as a mark of respect to him. I went back the country he had loved and encouraged me to explore initially and completed a trek to raise money in his name for the charity we'd discussed. I knew he would have approved and I was able to raise enough to put ten girls through school for one year.

It probably goes without saying that I found this trip physically, mentally and emotionally more taxing than the first as Adam's death was fresh in my mind and weighed heavily on my heart.

Every step of the way, I imagined him bounding from rock to rock ahead of me, fearless of heights and perfectly at home in the mountains. I missed him but being in a country he had felt such an affinity for made me feel closer to him and I noticed he sent me butterflies every day as I made the steady climb to above five and a half thousand metres yet again.

That had been the last long trip I had taken and as I thought about the solution I was looking for, images of Nepal kept drifting into my mind. I started looking at new treks in the region and was seriously considering attempting to walk the length of the Himalayas, even though I knew my health and fitness were not up to it at this point.

Grudgingly, I had to acknowledge that I wasn't physically or emotionally ready for a huge four month trek at high altitude. And so I started daydreaming instead about other locations. Perhaps I could go and learn Tai Chi in the mountains of China? Or I could head on the Vodka train from Beijing to Moscow? What about both? If I had a year off then, why not?

I have to admit I love planning vacations almost as much as the holiday itself. I remember researching the twelve month trip I had when I was twenty-one, and it hadn't exactly gone to plan, but hell it was a great adventure!

For the first three months in Africa, travelling with my mate Jim-Jam (James) from Kenya down to Zimbabwe, I couldn't exactly go wrong. We were on a travel package, which meant we joined about a dozen other people on a renovated truck that took us on a specific, planned route.

My parents thought I was mad as I'd hated camping as a kid and what I'd organised was three months of rough camping in Africa. However, I thoroughly enjoyed it, even the part where I wasn't able to wash for days at a time (it turned out to be good preparation for the Nepal treks).

The only bit I didn't like was going outside to the toilet in the middle of the night. I have a bladder the size of a pea, which meant this was a regular occurrence. A lot of the time we were 'free camping', which means not using campgrounds, so this could be quite an experience of being with nature.

In fact, one night it was a greater adventure than I would have liked. I was quietly doing my business behind a tree when a lion stalked by only several yards away. Both the lion and I literally stopped in our tracks as we assessed the situation.

I attribute my survival to my long red hair and lack of a shower as I think the lion must have considered me one of the same species and, therefore, strolled off nonchalantly. I was a little less blasé on my return to the tent than it was as it stalked off. After that I always made sure during my nocturnal wanderings that I stayed close to the fire.

After three months in Africa, I went to Australia where the rest of my planned twelve month trip went to pot. I'd always thought I would move to Australia permanently through work, but it turned out I got there through marriage instead, as I met, and fell in love with, Scott, who later became my husband.

Scott was, in my eyes, a handsome man in uniform, who seemed to want everything I did. When we met he agreed with me that he didn't want kids, he wanted to travel and, after we'd been married for a few years, even live in Europe. Actually now that I think of it, he agreed with pretty much everything I suggested, which should have caused warning bells!

Scott is a lovely man but his trying to make me happy by agreeing to everything I wanted caused trouble in the end. Once married, he became more comfortable in voicing his own wishes and desires, which turned out to be vastly different than mine. Whether intentional or not, he ended up changing his mind about almost all of our plans... I didn't.

After we got married and I moved to Australia, Scott left the Navy—which was a huge surprise to me—and we bought a house in Melbourne, where he seemed to think we would live happily for the next few decades as we raised our children.

As we struggled with the realities of married life and the financial struggles that every young couples faces, we had different perceptions of what was happening.

I have no doubt Scott was suffering too, but for me, being a long way from home and somewhat ill at ease with everything that was happening, my first couple of years of what was supposed to be wedded bliss turned into my own personal nightmare. I struggled to maintain my individuality and remember looking in the mirror one day, two years after being married, and not recognising myself.

Luckily, I had the courage to stick to my core beliefs and values and never gave in on having children, which would have ruined the rest of my life. Scott on the other hand had obviously realised he did want a family and saw earlier than I did that we needed to go our separate ways.

Having spent the first eighteen months of our marriage converting my legal qualifications, when I finally got back on the career ladder, I chose to enlist in the Army. I had learned lots about service life through Scott and it held a distinct appeal.

On the night we went out to celebrate my commission as a legal officer in the Army, Scott informed me that our relationship was over.

I cannot say it was a complete surprise as we had been drifting apart for months but, I certainly wasn't expecting it that night.

My commission was in Canberra so I moved there on my own to start my new career. It was a lonely time, but driving into work every day able to take in the view of the mountains in the distance helped.

Whilst I had been with Scott we had got a Border collie dog, Jessie, from the Society that protects animals in Australia. Mindful that she too was now lonely without me during the day, I rescued another dog, Jack, who turned out to be just what I needed.

He had come to me as damaged goods after being beaten as a puppy by the farmer I got him from. He needed me and I needed him.

A close bond formed between us that no one ever managed to break – despite a couple of boyfriends trying. I loved Jack and he loved me back unconditionally.

I admit it got a bit much when he started following me into the toilet and trying to jump on my knee whilst I was in there, so I did put some boundaries up!

Although he and Jessie slept in baskets and were not allowed on the furniture, they were effectively my only family in Australia and did become like my children. And, not surprisingly, Scott went on to have an actual child of his own.

Before we were divorced, while I was peace-keeping in a little country called Bougainville, the news arrived that he had a son. It was the one and only time that I can remember crying at work, and that was a huge shock to my colleagues since I'd endured a lot of pain during two crazy incidents on the first day I'd arrived and not shed a tear.

And that was how I'd ended up living in Australia.

In the end it had worked out alright. I'd gone from strength to strength in my career, moving from an Army officer to public servant to political adviser and eventually, after a winding road, to a lobbyist.

Actually, my journey into public service and working in Federal Parliament had come about through my putting to use back then the Positive Change Formula.

During my first trip with Scott to Australia's Capital, Canberra, back in the year 2000, we had visited Parliament House.

As I marvelled at the building and drunk in the air of power that diffused every pore of the place I was enamoured and realised I wanted to work there.

I stood on the roof of the building (a feat that is easier than it sounds as Australia's Parliament House is built into a hill) when I was still only converting my legal qualifications and declared that I would work there one day.

In following my formula I worked out that for me—a new resident of the country—the best way to do this was to get into public service and slowly work towards achieving my goal.

It was actually one of the key reasons I had looked into, and decided to join, the Army. Seeing Scott at work when we had been dating, I knew that it was my easiest foot in the door and enabled me to appreciate life as a public servant from the insider's perspective.

Having applied the formula and worked out the steps I needed to take, I rapidly moved from Army legal officer to public servant and climbed the ranks in a couple of government departments. Although I thought it would take me a long time to reach my goal, fate stepped in.

My reputation as a straight shooter, hard worker and someone who would provide frank and fearless advice was noticed by those up the chain of command and, in December 2004, I got a call from a Minister's Chief of Staff asking me if I would be interested in working in Parliament House.

It wasn't the way I envisaged it happening, but my goal was achieved nonetheless. Four years after I'd stood on the roof of Parliament House and announced my intention to work there, I was sat in the building advising Ministers.

Such is the power of intention and the Positive Change Formula! Why the hell I'd forgotten about it since that time is beyond me.

After reminiscing about the power of my formula, I got back to working out the solutions to the problems I was now facing in 2011. I set an intention to work out what I should do and let my brain percolate.

I know when I go to bed at night thinking about a problem I will usually wake up with the answer. In understanding this, I have a bad habit of waking up in the middle of the night with a head full of ideas—usually for work. I've adapted to this by keeping a notepad at the side of the bed so I can write everything down and then go back to sleep.

So, when I woke up at 2 a.m. I was as usual immediately wide awake with an idea in my head. I wrote down what I was thinking, which was just one phrase: *fifty dates in fifty states*.

I looked at it slightly puzzled, but now it was out of my head and on paper I turned off the light and went back to sleep. This was good since I needed to be awake for an important meeting in the morning.

When I woke up at 6 a.m. the next day, I immediately got on an overseas call to discuss various work issues with some colleagues. Over breakfast afterwards I looked at my notepad and chewed my toast thoughtfully as I considered what I'd written in the middle of the night.

Fifty dates in fifty states. I knew what it suggested, but could it really be a solution for my future—to date fifty guys in fifty states? That seemed crazy.

I tried to dismiss the idea, but had a nagging feeling that it was important. So, I looked at the number of goals it would potentially fulfil and subjected it to a pros and cons list.

If I were going to have fifty dates in fifty states it certainly upped the odds of my meeting a new life partner (Goal one). Given the time it would take, I'd have to quit my job and have time to consider what I wanted to do next in my life (Goal five). If I were going to quit my job I may as well have a couple of months with my family and good friends in the UK afterwards (Goals two and three).

Given that I would be exploring the US, I'd be doing a lot of travelling and a lot of walking, which would help me slim down and get fit again (Goals seven and four). And it certainly would be a break in my routine and one hell of an adventure (Goal eight). The only goal that I wouldn't attain was relocating to the countryside, but then again, the US had a lot of countryside I could visit while I was there, so in a way that goal would be achieved too.

I reviewed the list and went back to my other potential solutions. Hmmm, it was the one plan that hit all of my main goals. And more importantly... it just felt right.

With that analysis, I realised that what had at first appeared like a nutty idea now made perfect sense to me. My mind had presented me with the ideal way to achieve almost all of my goals in several months. So, in actual fact it would have been crazy not to embark upon the journey.

(By the way, if you managed to follow this chapter, you'll be great at mind-mapping because that's exactly how it works, jumping from one thought process to another!)

CHAPTER 5

Implementation

ith the solution in hand, I drafted a quick plan and set about implementing it with no further hesitation. I was resolved to keep the momentum and move forward.

I was excited, eager and full of enthusiasm for this new project. I'd found my reason to live again and, within a day, was feeling more confident, in control and happy—all through simply deciding what I wanted to change and how to make that change a reality.

My plan looked pretty simple on paper, but I knew from experience that the implementation phase could be difficult. The plan was as follows:

1. Sell the house.
2. Quit the job.
3. Find someone to look after the dogs.
4. Find storage for the car and furniture.
5. Book a flight to the US and organise accommodation for the first week in California.
6. Join US internet dating sites in order to find men to date on the trip and hopefully my Mr. Right.

7. Develop standard written questions to weed out the freaks, emotional fuckwits, creeps, married men and negative nellies. (I'd had my fair share of kissing frogs and thought this was the best way to reduce the odds of kissing any more).

8. Travel to all fifty US states and date a man in each.

9. Keep an open mind, beware of old, negative habits and try to avoid them.

10. Be kind to myself. Allow myself to grieve and to trust again. Learn acceptance and balance in order to reconnect with others and find new partner.

List in hand I got to it, immediately ticking the steps off one by one.

I remember clearly, I started on a Thursday afternoon, reaching for the phone book and dialling the real estate agent I'd bought the house from.

He had a photographer come out the next day. (Being anally retentive serves some purposes as my house was clean and I didn't need to do much to get it perfect for the photos!). The house was shown two days later on Saturday.

By Monday evening I'd negotiated the price I wanted for the house with an interested buyer and signed the contracts for sale. Before leaving work to meet up with the solicitor about the house, I formally resigned giving the company three months notice. I wanted to be fair to them and also provide myself enough time to complete the house sale, which usually took a minimum of eight weeks.

Scared of being distracted or talked out of my plan, I didn't wait around to see the reaction of the CEO or my boss. I pressed send on the computer and immediately got up and left, ready to set about the next stages of the plan.

After seeing the solicitor I went home and sent an email to my friends telling them what I'd done and what I was planning. I asked for volunteers to look after my dogs, car and furniture and, within a few hours, had homes for all of them.

This momentum seeded more. There was no stopping me now and no time like the present!

I set about the logistics of getting the dogs, car and furniture to Canberra, which was where the majority of my friends still lived. Thanks to the internet, I sorted out removal vans and was looking at flights, rental cars and how to find dates in the US that same night!

I printed a map of America and worked out a loose plan of where I would go and when.

Despite everything happening so quickly, I had the usual worries about travelling on my own for several months. I knew having a friend and some familiarity at the start of my journey would provide a buffer to these fears and so I wrote to my friend, Lorence, who lives in Los Angeles.

Given it was now late at night in Australia, it was daytime for Lorence, and I was surprised to find that he replied almost immediately with an open invitation for me to stay with him for as long as I needed.

I didn't want to impose for too long, but with my first few days sorted, I could start the trip with the knowledge that I had a friend to turn to if necessary. That was a great weight off my mind.

By the time I went to sleep that Monday night, I had sold my house, resigned from work, organised storage for my furniture and a home for the dogs, joined two dating agencies, worked out a rough route through the US and had a place to stay in the first week!

My plan was to leave in twelve weeks, spend three months in the US and take a side trip to Mexico for a two week rest just before my ninety day travel visa ran out.

From the US, I would travel to the UK to spend a few months—and Christmas—with my family. It would be my first Christmas in the UK for a decade and I was resolved to reconnect and heal some old wounds.

As an adult I wanted to gain their perception of events from my childhood and also to tell them what happened to me at sixteen and how it had affected me.

To me now, it is still amazing how everything happened so quickly and fell into place. From the Thursday to the Monday only five days had elapsed from the moment of decision to almost all of the logistics falling into place.

I had so much momentum that nothing could stop me! Or, maybe, I was afraid that if I paused, I'd change my mind.

In any case the next day, Tuesday, having joined the two US dating agencies late the night before, I decided I needed to add a profile and photos to try and capture the attention and interest of suitable men.

I admit I spent all of my lunch hour and a little extra hidden away drafting it. In the end my profile read as follows:

So... they don't have an option to be able to state upfront that I actually live in Australia at present. I grew up in the UK and Belgium and moved to Oz straight after university. I was only planning to stay a few years but my career took off and the country is wonderful so I stayed.

I am a five-foot nine redhead and a Taurus so allegedly I am fiery and stubborn—most people who know me nod in agreement when others point this out, so it could be true.

I am genuine, loyal and sociable. Depending on the circumstance and issue I can be flexible, open and easy going. However, if there is a moral question then I'm principled, stubborn and stick to my guns. Once I'm friends with someone I will do pretty much anything to help—I looked after a friends' sixteen year old daughter for half a year, which I have to admit was extreme! I am fiercely loyal but cross me twice and you will get short shrift—I am definitely not a doormat.

I love action and adventure movies but equally like a romcom with the girls. I enjoy the outdoor activities the countryside has to offer but love city work. Basically, I am not easy to pigeon hole or put labels on. I am my own person and not easily changed—I like who I am and am comfortable with myself. So if you are confident enough in who you are that you can cope with a girl who has her own opinions and likes a good debate, I would love to meet you.

O, and I can't emphasize too much just how much I LOVE travelling. I will soon be visiting the fifty states of America and will see where life takes me—maybe to your door and we can share new adventures together.

What kind of man am I looking for? Someone who is open, loyal and loving. A man who has confidence in himself and his own abilities and who doesn't get uptight if he dates a woman who earns more than he does. Someone who acts rather than simply talks and can be spontaneous and romantic. Smart yet down to earth. I'm not looking for perfection just a person I can trust and communicate openly with. :-)

Once finished, I called Miss G and asked her to come over that night. She had known about the house sale but I had so much more to fill her in on with all that had happened just in the last twenty-four hours.

Plus, I wanted to test the profile on her to make sure I was giving an honest portrayal of myself and to help clarify what I wanted in a man. Miss G tends to be extremely honest with me – sometimes too much so – and I knew if it passed her muster it was OK.

Despite thinking that the qualities I wanted in a life partner better reflected the personalities of my dogs than any guy I was likely to meet, she gave it the go ahead. Neither of us could argue that it isn't wrong to want loyalty, honesty and someone with an overall cheerful disposition in a world where those characteristics can seem so rare.

Another tick was added to my checklist.

I scanned the plan, six steps down, four to go.

Now for the standard questions.

Again I turned to my Miss G but now also included my other friends. I announced on Facebook that I was undertaking a social experiment by dating my way around the US and needed help with ten questions to weed out the nutters and give me the best possible chance of finding my Mr. Right.

The torrent of responses was amazing! After dealing with the first round of questions asking what the hell I was up to, everyone wanted to join me and everyone wanted to contribute a question.

It was pretty hard to just pick ten. But based on what I didn't want and what I was looking for, I picked the following:

1. Have you ever killed anyone or been to prison for any reason?
   With all the American crime shows exported to Oz, my friends had grave concerns that everyone in America was a serial killer or stalker. Personally I think this is in the same league as the question on immigration forms

asking if you are a terrorist... why the hell would anyone answer yes?! However, I kept it in just in case someone was stupid enough to answer in the affirmative.

2. Are you currently married/in a relationship and still with the person?

   This stems from the fact that my last fiancé turned out to have been married for the entire three years of our relationship... I told you I've kissed a lot of frogs! And I know, in hindsight I should have worked that out much earlier, how I didn't is a whole other story, mainly based on self-delusion.

3. Are you a member of a religious sect and/or do you speak in tongues?

4. Do you speak to your family?

   Although I'm not great at this myself, I'm assured men who have a good relationship with their families are the most stable and make better partners... hmmm maybe this says something more about me than them.

5. Do aliens ever speak to you?

   I've had a crush on David Duchovny since I was a teen and always imagined myself as Scully (well I have the red hair). So, if someone said yes to this question I think I'd have to date them.

6. What time of the day do you start drinking alcohol/ doing drugs?

   My American friends told me that this could be an important question, especially with people drowning sorrows caused by the economy and the downsizing of many American corporations.

7. Do you like to wear women's clothes/underwear?

   Again, this question was necessary thanks to an ex-boyfriend. I know some ladies may not have an issue with their partner donning their underwear but for me they are one item of clothing I don't want anyone else wearing, boyfriend or not!

8. Tell me ten random things about yourself.

   A friend of mine believes this is where people will unconsciously tell me a lot about themselves, so it's intended to get them to divulge their secrets and I wanted to see if it worked!

9. What three songs always get you singing.

I liked this question as I seem to have a song for most occasions so it would be interesting to know if they do too.

10. Name ten things on your bucket list and whether you have achieved them yet.

I thought this was a really neat question as not only will it expose whether we have similar interests, but it will also provide evidence of the other person's drive to fulfil their goals, or indeed, if they have any!

Another tick!

The next steps in my plan were the largest in the implementation phase. I would have a lot less control over them and, being a control freak, that scared and exhilarated me at the same time.

These steps were:

- Travel to all fifty US states and date a man in each.
- Keep an open mind, beware of old, negative habits and try to avoid them.
- Be kind to self. Allow myself to grieve and to trust again. Learn acceptance and balance in order to reconnect with others and find new partner.

I admit, I don't think this plan was what my dad had in mind when he reminded me of the happiness scale, which in turn made me remember the Positive Change Formula, but that's the joy of the equation—once you know what result you want it's amazing what the brain conjures up to get you there!

The Best Laid Plans...

Within a week of selling the house, resigning and working through the majority of the steps, I hit a bump in the road. I knew it would come but didn't expect it so soon nor in the form it came in.

My dog Jack stopped eating. Normally a glutton this was not a good sign and I rushed him next door to the vets, who, with me being their neighbour and Jack and Jess being daily over the fence acquaintances, rushed him straight in.

Within hours he had been operated on and I was told they had found and removed a huge lump in his bowel. They sent a sample for testing to confirm what they suspected – that my beloved Jack had an aggressive form of cancer. He was given a maximum of three months to live. I was devastated.

My dogs had been the reason I'd stayed in Australia and not given up and moved back to the UK after Scott and I divorced. I'd known it was a risk leaving two older dogs for a year but both had seemed so healthy that I stupidly thought they would last forever.

Now, just as I'd found them a temporary home with Daisy, Andrew and Kiara—long time friends in Canberra—and settled with my conscience having some time for me, Jack needed me more than he ever had.

The thought of leaving him when he was so sick was unbearable, as was the thought of putting him to sleep just because I had organised the trip. To me, he really was my little boy and having to say goodbye was heartbreaking.

It seemed ironic that just when I had finally accepted I needed to grieve for Adam, I had to grieve as well for Jack.

I could've taken this as a sign that I shouldn't go, especially as other parts of my plan had started to unravel too.

Work was pressuring me to rethink my decision and had offered me incentives to stay. I could finally be awarded the promotion I'd been promised more than a year before, together with the increased pay packet that went with it.

I could've pulled out of the house sale.

Everything was still in the stage where I could step back into my comfort zone... and a big part of me wanted to.

But I felt energised for the first time in years and I didn't want to lose that. I had fulfilled the first six steps so quickly it had seemed like the trip was destined to be. So I interpreted these problems as my conviction being tested. I looked again at my list and reminded myself where I was and where I needed to be to find happiness. Then I looked at Jack and knew what I had to do.

I compromised. I stuck with my plan but postponed the date of my leaving by another month. My work was mollified as they now effectively had four months to find a replacement and I knew that I would be with Jack for his final days.

While implementation can be difficult to see through, I knew the reward of fulfilling the changes I wanted would be worth it.

I wrote down in big clear letters what I wanted to achieve and stuck it on the fridge and, for good measure, put a smaller version inside my wallet.

Every time I felt my conviction wavering I looked at one of those pieces of paper and reminded myself that the alternative was unthinkable. I couldn't go on the way I'd been living and I knew I wasn't ready to give in without fulfilling whatever I was here to do. Somehow I just knew deep down that this was my path forward and no matter how hard it got I was going to stick with it.

Even so, twelve weeks later when I'd said my final tearful goodbye to Jack in the vet's surgery, I had a desperate urge to coil back into a ball and retreat to the life I had now become accustomed to. How could I go on and enjoy life with both him and Adam gone?

Inspite of my doubts, I pressed on and another four weeks later on Friday the 12th of August, I finished up at work, destined to get on a plane two days later to the US. I was in an absolute spin.

At the airport, I found myself writing to Adam as I generally do when I need extra guidance or just need to share how I feel. It was the 14th of August 2011, and I wrote the following:

O Adamski!

Bugger, bugger, bugger, bugger, shit!

What the hell was I thinking? What have I done? It's too late now. I already have twelve dates lined up thanks to my profile and regular visits to the internet dating sites to wink or flirt virtually with men. I'm going to board a plane to the US in a few hours and all of this planning is going to become a reality. What if I'm not ready to date? What if I'm still not ready to let you go?

Breathe, breathe, it's OK.

If I'm totally honest, I'd thought the house would be on the market for ages and was all prepared to change my mind if necessary. I still can't believe that this day has arrived.

I am here, four months after waking up with a crazy idea that seemed like the ideal solution. And now I have no job and no house but travel logistics in place and men lined up... and now I'm getting cold feet!

Maybe I've been listening to those friends who think I'm nuts to follow my dreams when Australia is starting to feel the knock on effects of the economic issues that the rest of the world is facing. Maybe the reality of it all is just beginning to sink in.

But here I am. Despite my pull to go back I need to move forward. I so desperately need the change and I am only hours away.

Wish me luck, Adamski!

Despite my trepidation, I got on that plane and, as soon as I buckled my seatbelt, felt a sense of calm. Again my plan just felt right and I allowed myself to relax into it and trust that feeling.

The Start of the 50 Dates
California

Unfortunately the feeling of calm didn't last. The most annoying family sat directly behind me and literally talked the whole sixteen hours of the flight. They were constantly getting up and down, knocking my seat each time as they went to chat with the rest of their extended family, who were in other parts of the plane.

When I arrived, I was exhausted from lack of sleep due to insufficient leg room and no privacy. I thought wistfully about the business class flights I'd taken with work. No more of those were going to happen any time soon and I was going to have to get used to it.

Despite jet lag and having to drive on the wrong side of the road, I made it safely to Lorences'. It was so nice to see a familiar face and have a place to crash until I found my feet.

Lorence looked just the same as when I met him on a cruise to Antarctica six years before. A little shorter than me and fine-boned with dark features, he was definitely cute but I don't think he knew it, or, if he did, modesty prevented him from showing it.

He was a doctor and exceptionally bright, and he knew facts about all sorts of random things. For example, did you know they have parrots in Pasadena? They're not native but he told me a guy brought them in illegally years ago and found out somehow he was going to get busted. To get rid of the evidence, he let them all go. As a result, there are parrots flying wild in L.A. I love little bits of trivia like that.

Although to me, parrots make sense in Pasadena, with its wide roads lined with palm trees, whitewashed houses and lawns that you just want to lie on because they look so clean and orderly. The mountains are hazy in the distance and it feels a world away from downtown L.A. with the grime, swarms of people and shops open twenty-four hours. I can understand why Lorence loves Pasadena.

When I arrived, Lorence took one whiff of me and sent me straight to the shower. He did so politely by offering me the facilities and gently encouraging me to use them.

When I turned up half an hour later in his lounge, which the Americans call a living room, I caught him up on what I was doing. Hearing that I had sold up and was travelling the US looking for love obviously came slightly out of left field to him and, just momentarily, a look of shock appeared on his face. I was glad he was sitting comfortably on his black leather sofa, otherwise, I think he would've fallen over in surprise.

Although he'd seen a happy side of me when I'd met him on holiday six years ago, he had gotten to know me over the past few years as a serious lawyer, political adviser and lobbyist. I reflected on how much I'd changed both in my eyes and everyone else's from the fun, adventurous person I used to be.

But now, I was back, and back with a vengeance!

Date #1: Chris – Life Is A Rollercoaster

My first date was arranged for the second day of the trip as my travel schedule was going to be packed. I had wanted to get underway as soon as possible, still wary that I could lose confidence and back out.

Given the timing, I also had to be conscious of jetlag and falling asleep on the guy, so I had suggested somewhere I knew I'd stay awake: Six Flags, Magic Mountain!

It's a theme park an hour north of L.A. and is known for having the most roller-coasters in America. I have to admit I'd been there twice before and it's my favourite theme park of all time so it seemed like the right place to start.

Looking back now, the ups and downs, being turned upside down, twirled around, feeling sick, exhausted, laughing, being energised and invigorated by the craziness of it all turned out to very aptly apply to my trip ahead.

My first date was with Chris, a six-foot African-American, who, at forty-four, was eight years older than me but didn't look it. He wore glasses and had one hell of a smile. He was a photographer and although it sounded as though his business had been hit by the lousy economic situation in the US, he could still smile and crack a joke... or seven.

I have to admit that from his texts and phone calls, he came across as a bit of an ass. Dry, sardonic wit doesn't really translate well in those modes of communication before you've actually met someone. I'd been wary of meeting him, but he'd agreed to my request for a day running around riding roller-coasters, so I figured he couldn't be too bad.

When we arrived there was a bit of an awkward moment as it appeared Chris felt obliged to pay. I put his mind at rest and told him I was up for going Dutch if he was OK with it and saw him breathe a sigh of relief.

I made a mental note to add that to the few dating guidelines I had already set myself, sensing that in America many of the men still have a traditional view that they need to foot the bill. For me, now used to paying my share, I felt just as awkward when a man insisted on paying.

So, I now had five guidelines, a list I was sure would grow as I travelled:

Safety first. Always drive myself and have dates in public and open spaces.

1. Set dates for venues suitable for travel clothes and be upfront with my dates that I will not be arriving dolled up to the nines.
2. No sex on the first date.
3. Kissing allowed.
4. Be ready to go Dutch when paying but equally be prepared to allow the man to pay if he insists and seems affronted by my approach.

I had no doubt these guidelines would get tested on my journey but felt it was good to have them anyway.

And I was quickly relieved I had allowed kissing as, several hours in, after going on all the fast rides at least once, Chris and I could be seen holding hands and literally running from one rollercoaster to the next.

After several hours of maximum adrenaline we stopped for a short break to fill up on the necessities – burger, fries, candyfloss and coke before running around again like excited children.

Chris being so crazy and hyperactive was just what I needed. And although I was attracted to him when he did move in to kiss me, I pulled back. Unsure why, I think maybe my subconscious was telling me there was no way I could maintain that kind of energy for long.

Chris had been a great first date, but wasn't 'the one' and I didn't want to give him any mixed messages by kissing him now. When we parted company around 7 p.m. that night I was genuinely happy to have met him and very grateful that he had been my first date. He had certainly got my trip off to a flying start... literally!

Resting up for a couple of days afterwards, I stayed with Lorence four nights in total before saying goodbye and heading to San Diego for a workshop.

The workshop was called *Three Days to Cash* and was run by Loral Langemeier and her company, Live Out Loud. I'd seen an advertisement for it in Sydney shortly after I'd resigned and being in the spirit of trying new things I'd signed up.

I'm not a person usually interested in entrepreneurial events, never having considered doing anything but working for other people. However, since I'd decided it was time for a few new experiences, I had gone along with an open mind and liked what I had seen.

Loral is tall, blonde, athletic, full of energy and a great orator able to read a room and build up the energy easily. I found out she is famous in the US for her Millionaire Maker series of books and workshops, helping people transition from working for others to working for themselves. I was intrigued so I had paid to go to this workshop in Melbourne, but when Jack got sick I changed to San Diego.

The idea behind the workshop is that you consider something Loral calls a *Cash Machine*, which can be a concept or innate skill that can be used to earn extra cash outside of a daily job. Then you have to actually sell that concept or those skills straight away at the event.

When I found that out in the first half an hour of sitting down in the room, I almost walked out again. I had no idea what I was going to sell. My legal skills and knowledge of the Australian political landscape were of little use in the US. Never having sold or marketed anything in my life I was daunted by the notion.

However, as I spoke to people and kept explaining why I was in the US, they absolutely loved the fact I'd given up everything and acted on my plan to date fifty guys in fifty states and try to achieve positive change in my life.

Everyone I spoke to thought it would make a great book and to prove it they bought it from me. I was surprised when at the end of the workshop I had made the most sales. The best part was coming out of my shell and feeling supported by strangers.

The energy and buoyancy I had felt from everyone's confidence in me during the workshop evaporated later when reality struck about what I'd signed up to do. I felt sick to my stomach. Who was I kidding? I wasn't an author.

At the event, however, with my new-found confidence and free spirit, I had also agreed to a date with the friend of one of the attendees. Why not, I had flippantly decided. I knew I was supposed to have fifty dates in fifty states and not all fifty in California, but the date would be good practice.

However, again, when it came to having the date, I felt a bit like I did about suddenly having to write a book. I wondered why I had agreed to it. *Shit.*

Date #2: Sam – Making Out At The Drive-In

On the way to meet my next date, Sam, I was cursing myself. When I first met him, I was a little disappointed by his appearance. But as the date went on and I got to know him, I felt a connection I hadn't felt in years.

Sam was thirty-one and exactly the same height as me. This was kind of weird as I'm used to dating men taller than I am, but I rationalised, if we ended up kissing later at least I wouldn't get a neck ache!

Originally from Mexico, he had chocolate brown eyes, thick black hair and tanned skin in a natural caramel shade that I could only ever dream of turning.

Over his right eye is a small scar and he has obviously broken his nose, which I found out later was due to a wrestling injury. You could tell through his light blue t-shirt that he had a good body, but I'd never have picked him as a wrestler because he didn't have those unsightly big neck muscles most have.

We caught up for lunch at a pizza place called 'Bronx' that was in one of San Diego's many suburbs. It was full of boxing and wrestling photos, which after finding out about his love for the sport made sense as to why he chose it.

Afterwards we drove to a cute little cake shop called 'Extraordinary Desserts', and I consumed my cake at a speed which I am sure is not ladylike. If I hadn't been on my best first-date behaviour, I'd have taste-tested the whole menu because it was delicious.

I found out later that had Sam not liked me that was where he had planned to end the date. However, instead, it was just the beginning.

We went to the Torrey Pines State Reservation for a walk along the cliffs above the beach. It's a pretty arid reserve with walks from inland to the cliff edge, and I believe you can walk down to the beach on one of the paths.

Having come out of a cold Australian winter I was still adjusting to the heat and conscious of not sweating too much when Sam told me what we could do, I opted for a steady stroll to the cliff edge to look out over the sea.

As we walked we talked about all of the things you are not supposed to discuss in polite company. We debated whether or not there was a God and the purpose of religion; we discussed politics and the state of the US; and we talked about ex relationships. Pretty heavy stuff for a leisurely stroll on a first date!

But when we stopped on the edge of the cliff and looked out, both of us fell silent. I'm used to seeing kangaroos on walks but here in front of me were whales and dolphins not far from the shoreline of the beach below.

Despite having seen these wonderful creatures before, their grace and beauty in their natural environment never ceases to amaze me. Sam stood quietly next to me taking in the sights and sounds as much as I was. The whole thing was delightful, and I had an overwhelming urge to kiss him right there.

I didn't have a guideline about whether I was allowed to make the first move or not, but I didn't want to ruin the moment. Being unsure whether that was what he wanted I held back, uncertain and suddenly self-conscious of my pale skin as it became shiny and red in the heat.

Although we'd walked at a slow pace, I could feel that my face was hot and sweaty from the afternoon sun. Red hair, pale English skin and humidity really don't mix. Even with all of my years in Australia which gets hot in the summer, unlike the UK, I will never be good in the heat.

After a lot of laughter, friendly banter and great debates about everything and anything we finally made it back to the car about 6 p.m. When Sam found out that I'd never been to a drive-in movie, we decided that we absolutely had to go to one... right now!

On the way we stopped off to buy some sandwiches to eat there. Images of Olivia Newton-John and John Travolta in *Grease* kept flashing across my mind as we drove.

I tried really hard not to talk during the movie as I know it drives people mad. But I really can't help it and don't know I'm doing it half the time. It's just that movies are so predictable, I feel compelled to utter the lines that I know will inevitably be said.

Sam had seen the movie before and thought it was hilarious that I was predicting lines and whole scenes. He wanted to know how the hell I was doing it.

I was enjoying the movie and Sam so much and then a typical 'Mel moment' happened. To describe a typical 'Mel moment', I'll give you an example.

As I mentioned earlier, I had joined the Army in Australia and gone peace-keeping in a country called Bougainville, which is off Papua New Guinea. On the first day there, exhausted after a week of arduous pre-training, we were made to do various exercises including a swim test and learning how to pop emergency flares. I have no idea why. Most of the time we were on solid ground rather than at sea and would never have any need to send up emergency signals from the middle of the ocean.

However, these were the exercises we had to do and I duly completed them—but not without incidence.

During the swim test I caught my wrist against some old, rusty metal stick out at the edge of the dock. The cuts were not very deep but would need treatment at the medical tent, I was told.

This being the case, I was ordered to go first during the next exercise and follow the instructions of the trainer in how to release an emergency flare.

I blame my tiredness and the fact that the instructor was a left-hander and I am right-handed for what happened next. (In truth though

I may have brains, but I really have no common sense so what happened was inevitable.)

As I followed the instructor exactly, I used my non-dominant hand and, consequently, instead of the magnesium flare singing joyfully into the air like a firework, I misjudged it completely and sent it flying painfully into my right wrist and directly into the open cuts.

The pain was excruciating and I think I must have gone into shock because I calmly looked at the instructor and asked for the directions to the hospital tent as I believed I really needed it now.

As there was no anaesthetic, the next thirty minutes of agony woke me up completely from the half-asleep state I had been in. I felt every bit of pain as the medic poured some form of acid onto my wrist to bubble the skin enough to scrub it and get rid of the burnt parts.

Since there was also a local man receiving treatment and I'd been told during cultural training not to swear in front of the locals, I could only very loudly exclaim 'Far out!' each time more skin was sloughed away. After being so politically correct, when I went back to my tent, which was only a few feet away, I shouted the other 'F' word a few times to get over the shock of it.

As if this wasn't bad enough, since I was only in a tent my voice carried farther than I imagined. I was very close to the mess (dining) area and everyone having dinner heard every word. For the duration of my rotation in Bougainville, I was known for this event.

I wish I could say it was the first and last 'Mel moment,' but, of course, it was not.

At the drive-in, partway through the film, I got hungry. So, I took one of the sandwiches we'd bought and bit into it. As I swallowed, I realised it had chilli in it, jalapeños apparently. Now, I know not many people are allergic to chilli, but I am.

Sam could tell straight away by my face that something was wrong, and, after trying surreptitiously to spit the rest out into a napkin, I explained my allergy and that I needed to head straight to the bathroom. I hoped he would stay in the car, but as a gentleman he felt compelled to join me. O the shame!

Ducking and weaving through the parked cars and trying not to get in the way of the film for the other patrons, I made it quickly to the bathroom and sent Sam to get some water as I didn't want him to hear me throwing up. I needed to get the chilli out of my system quickly and fend off any reaction.

A few minutes later, fingers still down my throat and coughing up the last remnants of anything that remained in my stomach, I was mortified to hear Sam's voice calling quietly to me from outside the bathroom to see if there was anything he could do.

The poor guy was standing outside the ladies toilets listening to his date vomit. Seriously, is it just me this kind of thing happens to? A romantic evening had turned into a farse!

I thought it was all over from there but Sam was made of sterner stuff. In fact, when we got back to the car and I filled him in on what we'd probably missed, he jokingly said the next time I got a prediction right I'd get a kiss.

Yuck! I'd just been sick and although I'd downed two bottles of water and gargled, the last thing I wanted to do was kiss someone. I couldn't resist the temptation, though, and predicted another line.

'That's it!' he said in mock anger and leaned across and kissed me.

Despite being so self-conscious of how unromantic it must be to kiss a girl who'd just chucked up, during the kiss he managed to make me forget all about it.

I enjoyed kissing him so much that I purposely predicted another line and got another kiss for my amazing movie predicting ability.

During the kiss, in the child-like fashion that I used to be known for by my family and friends before Adam's death, I had a giggling fit. I couldn't help it. I've always wanted to go and 'make out' at a drive-in.

The problem was the kissing started when the movie was ending but, after I stopped giggling, Sam told me we were in luck as it was a double bill.

So... we kissed throughout the interlude and through the start of the next movie. And we kissed until it got to the stage when it might no longer be a PG-rated scene. At which point I suggested that perhaps there'd been enough kissing for one night and I needed to head home.

When I woke the next day I was so happy I literally jumped out of bed and into the shower. Sam and I had agreed to meet for breakfast before I started my drive to Phoenix, which was due to get underway that morning.

Because I didn't want to miss his call, I placed my phone on top of the toilet so I could hear it. No call came and I hopped out of the shower and went to grab the phone. A normal manoeuvre for most people but, for me, as the world's clumsiest person, it turned into a fiasco. The phone went flying off its perch and landed in the toilet bowl.

I can't imagine that anything would like swimming in a toilet bowl and my phone was no exception. When I fished it out I dried it gently, blew on it, talked nicely to it and then pleaded with it. I even gave it a little massage but to no avail. My phone was dead and not coming back.

Great. I couldn't remember Sam's phone number, my iPad had no battery and I had no idea how to tell him what happened or where I was. I did what anyone would do in my position. I panicked and my mind went blank.

Although I knew the shops were still closed, I drove around in vain looking for a store that sold mobile phones so I could try and retrieve the information. But to no avail.

The time for my departure came and went and I hung on but knew I couldn't stay much longer. I found a little Internet cafe and emailed what I remembered was Sam's email address to apologise for being a total klutz and hoped that he would forgive me. And then there was nothing else I could do. I had to leave.

The rest of the day things just got worse as I totally humiliated myself at the petrol station because I couldn't find the lever to open the petrol cap. I sat reading the manual for ages only to find that it opens simply by pulling the flap on the cap.

Then I couldn't work out how to use the pump since in the US you have to pay first... who knew?! After fifteen minutes of watching me talk to myself in the car and then standing at the pump gesticulating wildly in frustration, the attendant must've been getting worried because he came out to see if I was a complete lunatic or just another foreign tourist.

Driving the US highways became another lesson in cultural differences. Based on the several hundreds of people on the road it seemed the standard road rules in Europe and Australia didn't apply – at least not in California.

Whereas I grew up with the mantra: mirror, signal, manoeuvre (MSM), it appeared to me that the average American driver relied on extrasensory perception (ESP) to know when to pull out or move across lanes. On too frequent an occasion, ESP didn't work. I was cut across not twice but three times, which meant I had to honk my horn to fend off prospective crash scenarios.

When I indicated, it seemed to be the signal for the person to speed up and stop me getting across rather than letting me in. And leaving even a horse hair of a gap between me and the person in front was an invitation for someone to cut in front of me. I've never had to brake so hard and so often.

Having to slow down quickly into a near traffic jam seemed a common occurrence, strangely enough because of rubbernecking by car drivers who wished to view an accident caused by other drivers who didn't leave a gap and relied on their not quite so failsafe ESP!

Californians are allegedly the most laid back of all Americans, but when it comes to driving they are vicious!

Except for those people who drive in the fast lane. It seems that the fast lane is not used for overtaking in California, it is instead the slow lane. From what I could see you can just pick any lane when you get onto the highway and then... stay there. Not doing the speed limit? Out for a Sunday drive? O well I'll just sit in the fast lane and impede everyone else's journey!

I'm not sure whether it was because I was still upset at myself for the phone incident and missing Sam but everything just proved to annoy me even more.

I have to admit that I tried a few tricks to see if I could get the person sauntering along in the fast lane to move across but nothing worked. Zooming up behind them at breakneck speed and slamming on the brakes or following them closely got no reaction or change of lane whatsoever. It was frustrating to say the least.

To calm my frayed nerves I came up with an ingenious new game I dubbed, 'Car Tetris'. I'd scan the four or five lanes ahead, calculate the speeds and gaps between vehicles and then move from one lane to the next. Moving across all lanes and back again got extra points.

Not the actions of a normally rational and professional lady but needless to say, it turned an otherwise frustrating, steer-wheel biting, tedious drive into heaps of fun... and I arrived in Phoenix much faster than Randy (the name of my new American GPS) anticipated and in a much better mood than when I left.

Arizona

As I drove across the country, the terrain changed to dry arid dirt, rocks, the occasional mountain and the even more occasional tree. Instead of its taller plant cousin, Saguaro cacti had taken root, and the land was literally littered with them, standing like men with their arms held up in surrender.

Given my early arrival for my date, I had time to replace my phone; however, that didn't help me retrieve Sam's number. My sim card was hopelessly dead. So I ducked into a McDonalds to make use of their free electricity and wifi. When my iPad finally had enough juice for me to check my emails I was trying not to get my hopes up that he would've replied. After all, the email address could have been wrong, he might not have checked it, or he may not want to answer anyway.

A mixture of emotions swirled as I opened my account, scanned through and there it was... a reply! I was ecstatic! I opened it and read quickly. Then I read it again, letting the information sink in. O God. The poor boy.

Not only had he called, and called, and called, but he'd left work and driven forty minutes to the town where I was staying in the hope that I was asleep or in the shower and would answer by the time he got there. Then he drove around, trying to work out which hotel I would be in.

Apparently, as he works in overalls on a building site, he'd changed into clean clothes in his car and gone to a restaurant for breakfast and kept ringing.

He said he drove back to work dejected, wondering what had happened and whether he'd done something wrong. He thought of hundreds of reasons why I didn't answer, but none of them included a swimming phone. However, he joked, having seen me in action, he wasn't sure why this wasn't the *first* reason that had come to mind.

I replied and sent him my number in the hope he would call, and, in the meantime went on another date with, Diego who was, believe it or not, another Mexican who had decided to move permanently across the border.

Date #3: Diego – Allergies And Rock Concerts

Diego was driving up from Tucson, which is just over an hour south of Phoenix. I'd been talking to him for more than a month and he was a personal favourite of mine.

Granted he wasn't what you'd call good-looking in a traditional sense. He looked a bit like a nerd in his photos with his bookish glasses. But I have to wear glasses too, on occasion, and can also be classed as nerdy, so I thought I shouldn't judge him before knowing him.

Also, his emails were great. He managed to be witty, charming, self-deprecating and gentlemanly in just a few paragraphs.

While planning my trip, I'd noticed that Def Leppard was playing in Phoenix at the same time I'd be there. Def Leppard was a band of my youth and reminded me of having fun with the group of lads I used to hang out with. It was a time before I really had anything too serious to worry about. So I'd asked if Diego wanted to join me and, even though it wasn't his thing, he'd agreed.

An hour after meeting him, however, I wondered if someone else had written his emails for him as the witty repertoire I was expecting was sadly lacking.

He also told me that I'd got the date wrong and the Def Leppard tickets we had were actually for the next day. That meant I had to spend an extra twenty-four hours with him, which was especially awkward as my friend from Australia, Rachael, was arriving in the morning, so there would be three of us.

The only thing that seemed to go right for me that day was when I retired to my room and got a surprise call from Sam. We spent more than an hour on the phone together, giggling at how my day had panned out. He helped me put it all into perspective and lifted my mood.

He knew that I was dating guys in every state and seemed to be pragmatic about it. After all, we'd only been on one date. He said he just wanted me to have fun and keep him posted. I was worried that meant he was not interested in me, but he put my mind at rest and told me that when I managed to got back to California, we'd have our second date.

When Rach arrived the next morning, I spotted her immediately as she strolled through the airport... all five-foot ten of her. Tall and elegant despite her travel clothes and mussed hair that looked as though she'd tried to sleep but hadn't managed it, she handled with her usual aplomb the fact that I had a short, chubby man in tow.

Rachael is the consummate professional public servant, diplomatic yet sharp as a tack. We met five years before when I worked at the Minister's office. She was my go-to girl in the department and often provided me with invaluable assistance in the manic minutes before question time when we needed information urgently.

Question time, as any political hack will tell you, is supposed to be where Ministers seriously debate the issues of the day and what to do about them. Most Ministers arrive armed with files full of facts and figures about certain crime rates, or the number of patients in their local hospital, or what projects they have funded to reduce the incidence of speeding in inner cities.

It is supposed to be instructive, serious debate. Unfortunately, these days in most parliaments around the world, all you will find is a show where Ministers bray and guffaw at each other and try to score points.

Watching question time sometimes made me wonder why I was working so hard in the first place. But then I would look at the Ministers I knew personally and my friends in government departments who, for years, had worked tirelessly to create positive change for all Australians, and I would find the will to carry on.

So Rachael's professionalism as she met Diego was a reflection of her character yet again. A couple of years older than me, you wouldn't guess it from her general appearance. However, when it came to having her shit together, Rachael was streets ahead!

She not only had a great job but also the most wonderful husband, Simon, who was blonde, blue-eyed and handsome, laid back, intelligent, trustworthy *and* trusting.

He didn't bat an eyelid when, after a walk, I had managed to convince Rach to join me for two weeks to re-enact Thelma and Louise's adventures across the US of A.

And Rachael didn't ask for permission. She just told him that was what she wanted to do and he was happy for her.

No power struggles, no 'why not with me', nothing. He is the perfect man in my book and, given Rach is such a wonderful person, they are the ideal couple. When imagining the kind of man and relationship I want, theirs is definitely what I hoped to find and emulate.

When I introduced Rachael to Diego, she smiled genuinely, and the three of us headed to Sedona for a walk to wake her up and allow her to stretch her legs after twenty-four hours of sitting on planes.

Being the local, I was happy enough to let Diego drive my rental car now Rachael was with me, but soon regretted it as I found that he was among my least favourite American drivers—the ones who sit in the fast lane going way below the speed limit.

When we got to Sedona, Rach and I were blown away by the strangely shaped red rocks that surrounded us and appeared at times to glow when the sun hit them at a certain angle.

Again the ground was dry, but there were small trees and bushes strewn across the landscape, so it didn't look completely barren.

We explored the Chapel of the Holy Cross, which was built on top of and into one of the many thousand-foot, red-rock formations around, and appeared to rise out of it. It was an impressive building, but to me it could in no way compare to the natural majesty of the area.

Sedona reminded me greatly of the centre of Australia around Uluru (also known as Ayer's Rock) and the Olgas. There, as here, the vastness of the landscape is breathtaking.

I stood and marvelled at the humans, who must have crossed this area on foot or horseback centuries before. Even on my most adventurous of days I certainly wouldn't want to attempt a journey out here and risk getting lost wandering around in the heat. An air conditioned car and bit of a walk along a marked path was sufficient for me, thank you.

We must have all had a similar feeling since, as we stood outside the chapel taking in the view, we unanimously decided that a short, marked trail was just the ticket rather than getting hot and flustered clambering around in places we shouldn't go.

Down the trail, we soon found ourselves beside a stream and amongst the big rocks. It was relaxing and the sun was shining so we should all have been enjoying ourselves. However, the conversation was strained and, I'm ashamed to say, I found myself talking mainly to Rachael about what she'd been up to since I had left and our plans for the next two weeks.

Diego was getting quieter and quieter, so I tried to include him more in the conversation but to no avail. After a while I noticed he was a shade paler than when we had left, which was odd as it was hot and he really should have been flushed with the heat. So, I suggested we turn around and he readily agreed.

We headed to a cafe for a late lunch and, by now, Diego really didn't look well. Rach and I kept looking over at him in a concerned fashion as, not only was he going green, but he also appeared to hold his food in the side of his mouth like I've seen rodents do on occasion as they break between chews.

I looked quizzically at Rachael, who'd noticed this too. We both kept staring at him as he filled up his mouth with food that he managed to somehow hold in the side pockets of his cheeks whilst he talked – and then chewed. The sight of half chewed food remnants seemingly being held like washing suspended between spin cycles was not pretty but, as with a train wreck, we just couldn't seem to look away.

After a while he noticed me staring so I felt compelled to tell him that he was looking ill and asked whether he felt OK. It turned out he suffered from allergies especially when exposed to grasses etc, so the walk had made him sick! I am sorry, but if he knew that why the hell did he suggest it?

The great thing was that, at this juncture, Rachael kindly volunteered to take his place at the Def Leppard concert should he not feel up to it. I crossed my fingers... He thought about it for the entire journey back to the hotel (which with me driving took a lot less time) and finally said he was too sick and just wanted to go back to Tucson. I gave him the money for his ticket and Rach took his place.

I could not have asked for a better date! I'd never seen Rach on a night out as we've always been work and dog walking buddies, but now I've seen another side to her... I liked it.

Mild-mannered public servants by day—rock chicks by night! Turns out we had a lot more in common than I thought and both loved '80s and '90s rock.

We had the best time and, although, I felt a pang of guilt for poor Diego, I couldn't help but be grateful for his allergies. It just would not have been the same eating hotdogs, drinking beer and head-banging to *Pour Some Sugar On Me* with anyone other than my mate, Rach.

Since we both loved to hike, the next day we headed to the Grand Canyon with the intention of hiking down and walking back up. However, once we got there and peered over the precipice into the great abyss, I'm pleased to say that, for a change, good ol' common sense took over and we decided it might be better to ask how long it normally takes and whether provisions were necessary.

The answer was two days with an overnight at the bottom and an eight hour hike back to the top. As we were only staying two days, we opted for an easy walk along the top and a scenic helicopter flight through the canyon instead. Since leaving Oz, I really was not getting the exercise that I should!

As we walked I couldn't help but think of Adam, who would have loved the place. The rocks, the colours, and the scale of it. Nature truly is amazing. No human could ever have made something as spectacular.

Adam would've been running around, jumping across rocks and scaring me senseless. Thinking of him with the long dark brown hair that he had when we dated all those years ago, I could imagine him frolicking from one area to the next with his pony tail bouncing around wildly behind him.

If he were with me, people surely would have mistaken him for a Native American and asked him about the history of the place. Which, knowing Adam and his penchant for reading up about all the places he travelled to, he would have been able to quickly answer.

Despite jumping out of planes, abseiling and climbing mountains, as Adam at times cajoled me and at others inspired me to do, I've never gotten over my aversion to heights. I was slow and careful while Adam was as fearless and agile as a bloody mountain goat. I could never keep up.

As we walked along the path, I couldn't help but talk about him to Rachael.

The funny thing is, although I'd known Rach for years, she really didn't know anything about why I made the sudden flight back to the UK when Adam died and then was gone for a month. She told me she'd often wondered why, when I returned, that I left again to start afresh in Sydney with a new job.

I explained to her all about my childhood crush and how Adam and I actually starting dating after bumping into each other again at a nightclub when I was home from university.

I spoke of all of his endearing as well as annoying qualities. About the reason I had left him in the end, which was partly because he had cheated on me but mainly because he'd become so reliant on me in many other ways that I felt simply unable to provide for him all I believed he needed.

I remembered how we always had a knack of knowing when the other needed help and an uncanny ability to reach out just at that time.

Even on the day he died I had called and left a message on his parents' answer-machine because he was on my mind.

I laughed while reminiscing about our holidays to India and Egypt and was a little embarrassed when admitting my anger that when he came to stay with me in Australia years after we had gone our separate ways, he still hadn't appeared to let go of a lot of the pain from his past. He still seemed to want me to sort out his problems somehow.

Rachael listened and asked questions and it was a release of sorts to talk openly about him and our relationship and my feelings for him.

'I really believe that, if he had lived, when I got back to the UK to surprise him we might have sorted things out finally. I don't know about him but I was ready to try and make a real go of it. I'd always loved him and his being ill had made me realise how much.' I admitted as tears of hurt, anger and regret spilled down my cheeks and clouded my view of the landscape as we walked.

Rachael, sensing my need now to talk privately found a quiet spot and gently steered me to it. We sat on the cliff edge, legs dangling over the side as I stared blindly out at the Canyon below.

'He died several weeks before I got to see him again and find out.' I choked, as I spoke between shallow, heavy breathes.

'Why did I never know about this?' Rachael asked quietly.

'I know I can be loud and confident at work, but my private life is an area I don't usually talk about given it's normally a disaster.' I confessed, turning to her and looking up at her cautiously from under my tear-laden eyelashes. 'Adam and I were both pretty private and I don't think anyone around us really knew where we were at in our relationship. When he died it seemed somehow inappropriate to bring it up when so many others were suffering his loss too.'

I let out a shuddering breathe. 'I was left with so many questions: Would we have got back together? If he'd known I was coming, would he have somehow clung on? Had he told anyone how he was feeling about me so I could find out? I was unable to share these questions with anyone and I guess I started drowning in my grief. When I left Canberra it really was the start of my spiral down into severe depression.'

'I wish you had told me, Mel.' Rach whispered as she put a comforting arm around my shoulders.

We sat for about five minutes in silence and then I told Rachael something that I had never really articulated. 'I think Adam would be really proud of me for taking this trip.' I said. 'He would have loved the idea of my travelling again and been happy in the knowledge that I had finally realised there was more to life than work'.

'From what you have said, I have no doubt you're right.' Rachael replied as she squeezed my hand gently.

Sharing this with Rachael at the top of the Grand Canyon, was the first big step in my opening up and reconnecting with myself and others. It was scary, but Rach was understanding about it all as I knew in my heart she would be.

That night I wrote to Adam:

Hi Adamski,

I felt like you were with me today as I spoke about you to Rachael. I know you would have been loving the Grand Canyon and soaring over the rocks.

I miss you.

I have so many things I still want to talk to you about and to ask you but I know I have to let those and you go at some point. I think I am getting closer to that day, Adam, but I want you to know that no matter what I will never forget you.

I don't want to replace you my darling Adamski, that's impossible. But, I do want to be able to open my heart and allow someone to love me again.

I am so scared of feeling this pain all over with someone new. The idea of dating and splitting up with a guy no longer scares me, but, the idea of loving a man who later dies terrifies me.

How do I reconcile those feelings with my desperate desire to find somebody to share my life and love with?

I'm looking to you, Adamski, to guide me on this crazy journey. I am following your example of living life to the max and doing away with the traditional rules we live by. Don't let me down, I'm counting on you.

New Mexico, Texas, Oklahoma, Arkansas

On the way to Albuquerque, Rachael and I drove part of the old Route sixty-six Highway. Historic signs still point the way here and there with motels and diners that looked like they hadn't been renovated since the 1950s and reminded me of the old Elvis movies I used to watch with my Aunty Barb occasionally when I was still living in the UK.

Up until this point I'd been booking hotels days ahead of schedule; however, in an effort to try and save money, I'd opted for a website that hosts bed and breakfasts.

Unfortunately, the one I wanted was unavailable, so I called on my next date, Nathan, for his advice and booked a hotel through a website he recommended.

By following Nathan's instructions to the letter, I ended up in the same hotel where he was staying. He apparently lived out of town and had come in for the date.

In fact, Nathan was waiting at the hotel when Rach and I arrived and suggested we go out for dinner ahead of our date the next day. Feeling hot and tired but beholden to him, I reluctantly agreed. Having already had to endure one of my dates, Rach politely declined and left me to it.

Since New Mexico was conquered by the Spanish and belonged to Mexico until 1912, I half-expected to be dating someone of Mexican descent, but Nathan was a Brit. He was about five-foot eleven with an average build, and had mousy-coloured hair that was just beginning to turn grey and typical British features—pale skin, green eyes.

In our prior communication over the web, he had seemed like a great guy. We obviously had a lot in common having both moved permanently to new countries, and we had conversed easily. He had definitely been on my top ten list and I'd been hoping I hadn't misjudged him as I had Diego... but I was wrong again.

Date #4: Nathan – Scary Stalker Material

It wouldn't be an exaggeration to say that Nathan had called me more than a dozen times over the past two days—a difficult feat given the problems with mobile reception at the Grand Canyon! After we sorted out the hotel when I was still on the road heading his way, I told him where I was and we established I was fifteen minutes away. He then texted me three times more before I arrived. Who does that!

And when we met, I was allowed only ten minutes to get to the room, shower, change and head back out again before our extra date. Again, because I was feeling beholden to him I didn't stand up for what I needed, which was rest, instead I succumbed to his pressure.

Within five minutes of being alone with Nathan I knew it was going to be a long night! I can chatter with the best of them but I had nothing on this guy. I reckon he could talk under water with marbles in his mouth!

I wouldn't have minded if it'd been interesting but it wasn't particularly. When he did stop long enough for me to make a comment, as soon as I started speaking he got an annoyed look on his face, which gave me the impression he wanted to hit me. It was very disconcerting, which is probably what he wanted so I would shut up and he could talk some more.

When we got to the restaurant for dinner, he told me that we were in a part of town called Nob Hill. Apparently it was a chic part of town where the 'in-crowd' hangs out.

Now feeling annoyed, agitated and no longer in any way beholden to Nathan, and having never been interested in belonging to an 'in-crowd' nor in status or material goods, I wanted to tell him that the only 'nob' I could see was him. And I might have done so if I had been able to get a word in.

For me the highlight of meeting Nathan was learning about the online hotel booking service, so you can guess how riveted I was by the conversation. When we got back to the hotel I was trying to get to my room but he kept me in the lobby trying to take control of the logistics for the rest of my trip.

I was getting tired and more than a little concerned about his intense interest in where I was going and what I was doing. So, I placated him with an agreement to meet up the next morning for breakfast before our date so we could talk about it more.

I'd been looking forward to wandering around Albuquerque's old town as I'd heard it was like being in Mexico and very different than much of America with the architecture being of Spanish and Mexican origin. I noticed that many of the people spoke Spanish and the place names clearly demonstrated their heritage.

I really had been looking forward to learning more and enjoying the different atmosphere this state had to offer. However, now I was dreading it with the thought of having to spend more time with Nathan.

I usually have good instincts about people, and all of my alarm bells were ringing after the date. Having relied so much on my ability to read people in the past, I normally take heed when my intuition tells me something is wrong, and have learnt from experience that not listening can be dangerous.

When I got to the room I spoke to Rachael and she agreed that after his obsessive ringing and texting, trying to take over my logistics, and getting me to stay in the same hotel as him, he was indeed scary, stalker material. We made a plan to depart very early the next morning and determined I would not waste any more time or get myself in deeper with such a person.

I left Nathan a note at reception with a lame excuse as to why we had to leave, and we hot-footed it out of there. Not wanting to jinx any of my living relatives, I cited the death of one long passed and the need to find an international flight out of Texas.

This did not stop Nathan calling and texting me for weeks after our date – needless to say except for the first call where I apologised and stuck to my excuse, I refused to answer and never spoke to him again!

Dates #5&6: Dylan & Tom – Vegetarians And Memorials

My next few dates didn't really get any better. I managed to choose the only vegetarian in Texas for my date there and, whilst I have absolutely nothing against vegetarians, I was hoping to have a true Texan cowboy experience. Rach and I made up for this with a great big steak dinner though.

This was followed by a date with a guy in Oklahoma I can't even remember the name of because he bored me senseless (although the Oklahoma City Memorial is the best I've ever seen and was well worth the visit).

Date #7: Josh – Another Ex-Girlfriend On The List?
And finally there was my date with Josh, a CEO in Arkansas. We enjoyed a few beers together in the pub he suggested after I told him dinner at a posh restaurant was a no-go because I only had jeans and travel clothes.

When I arrived, he was already waiting. At six-foot three he was tall, broad, muscular with blonde hair, sparkling blue eyes, a wide smile and perfectly white teeth that seem to be a prerequisite for life in America.

His casual clothes were Calvin Klein jeans, a light-blue, open-necked Tommy Hilfiger shirt that set off his blue eyes perfectly and brown loafers that were probably a very expensive label too. Casual but definitely classy.

I held my head up high and greeted him with what I hoped was an equally engaging smile.

The few hours we spent together started off well. He was clearly a smart, articulate, charming and engaging man, which reminded me of an American president who had hailed from the same area. I just hoped he didn't have other similar traits.

He was clearly a family man and spoke often and fondly of his three children. Although kids are not really my thing, it's not because I don't like them, it's just that I have no maternal instinct or wish to be tied down to such an extent.

Some people do, some people don't, and I was in that bucket of people. As a female it is a difficult place to be. It is still society's expectation that all women should procreate so something must be seriously wrong or defective with you if, as a woman, you don't go all gooey and clucky at the sight of a baby.

Obviously, Josh already having three children would not, I hoped, need to expand his brood any further, which from my point of view was a good thing.

So the fact he had kids was, as far as I was concerned, a bonus. They were all in their early teens, an age I can cope with, so it was perfect!

And, understanding their importance to him and the bond between parents and their offspring, I made sure to remember their names as Josh told them to me and showed me their photos from his wallet.

I am very good at remembering names and faces, a skill I honed when working with Ministers in Parliament. It turned out to be a useful tool that I naturally managed to develop out of my genuine interest in people.

This small, subtle acknowledgement landed, as I'd hoped it would, and Josh probably opened up more than he normally would on a first meeting.

He confided in me the issues he was having with his ex-wife and then started talking about his ex-girlfriend and her flaws as well.

I nodded and listened and obviously gave him the impression of understanding and empathy. However, in the back of my head I was imagining him having this conversation with a future date about me, if I were to actually become his girlfriend – and no doubt ex-girlfriend!

What had started as friendly banter had gradually turned into him slagging off his exes, and then, more scarily, he started asking me probing questions in what I felt was an effort to see if I would be a suitable replacement and potential stepmother.

At the end of the date, he expressed an interest in spending more time together, so I'd obviously passed his test, but he certainly hadn't passed mine.

I wrote to Adam to complain:

Come on, Adamski! I know you like a joke, but this is getting ridiculous! I can almost hear you giggling over my shoulder as each date unfolds. What are you trying to tell me here, I should give up? Throw me a bone, will you? I deserve a good date after surviving the last few!

I sat back after writing it and reflected. What each date had proved to me was that the connection I'd made with Sam was a rare thing that

I shouldn't take lightly. We'd been on the phone almost every night, laughing about my adventures.

Travelling was proving to be a great way for me to get to know Sam in a slow, relaxed manner without the need to jump into bed with him or rush into things. Also helping was a game I'd bought at the Oklahoma Memorial. *Choices* had probing questions such as, *If you could only fly or walk for the rest of your life, which would you choose and why? If you could only have one arm or one leg, which would you choose and why?* It was through his answers to 'why' that I was learning more about his views on life and our different values in some cases.

I found myself looking forward to talking to him every night and sharing with him the hilarious details of the dud dates.

Hmm... I knew what that suggested.

Tennessee

I can't remember when my working relationship with Rachael turned into friendship or who first suggested a weekend walk together, but through our regular contact we developed a close and trusting relationship. And I am so glad she allowed me to talk her into joining me on my adventure.

And whilst I was playing the *Choices* game with Sam at night, I was playing the *Denny's* game with Rachael during our long drives.

I'd created the Denny's game to keep Rachael and I amused on our drive across the country from West to East. It's an easy game and Rachael and I became highly competitive about it.

Basically the first person to spot a Denny's sign gets one point. The person to spot the actual restaurant gets two points. If you called 'Denny's' but the restaurant or sign turns out to be something else (there are lots of restaurants with the same colour scheme so it happened quite frequently) a point is deducted. The person with the most points at the end of the day wins.

The game proved really useful for keeping us awake during some of the longer hauls along Eisenhower's Interstate Highway System, which could be extremely tedious given the roads were so boringly straight.

Apparently, President Eisenhower had based the system on Hitler's autobahns after watching the Germans move military equipment so quickly around the country during the war. Great for speed – and as Rach and I both found out – speeding tickets!

Rach had taken the brave step in getting behind the wheel after Texas and we were now happily sharing the driving, making quick progress as it turns out we are both lead foots and normally sit a little bit over the speed limits. This meant we were getting across the country quicker than we thought but it was also creating a dent in both our wallets as we also both managed to get pulled up for speeding in quick succession.

As well as a love of speeding along the open road, it turns out Rach and I also shared a love of an eclectic array of music, including Blues, Jazz and... Elvis. So, when I told her Memphis was our next stop, she insisted that we visit Beale Street and Graceland and I didn't exactly need any arm twisting to agree.

Graceland, the home of Elvis! I'd heard so much about it from my Aunty Barb, who adored him and had Elvis paraphernalia everywhere.

Aunty Barb was my favourite Aunty. She was slender with grey hair, which was always curled either with a perm or rollers. Her crinkly and well-worn face, gave her a kindly look, which had an uncanny ability to turn hard as stone if someone upset her or her family! After my Nanna died, she became the matriarch of the Brocklehurst clan and knew what was going on with every one of us. If you'd listen, she would talk proudly about us all for hours at a time.

She was my dad's older sister and the twin of my Uncle Mel. Yes, my namesake as the other Mel Brock in the family. Aunty Barb had a dry sardonic wit and a love of hugs and having her back scratched—genes that many of us in the family inherited. Her house was always spotless and she refused to go out without her hair looking perfect. Until my teens, she had me believing that she was a brain surgeon when, actually, she was a cleaner at the hospital.

Almost thirteen years before, I'd walked down the aisle to Elvis' *Only Fools Rush In* especially for her, which brought her to tears. Little did I know how accurate that particular song would be in respect to my short-lived experience of married life!

So, when I arrived at Graceland I felt in some way that Aunty Barb would be walking around with me, giving me commentary. She had told me all about her pilgrimage there with my dad and their respective other halves now over a decade before. For her Graceland was hallowed ground.

I couldn't resist ringing her and telling her where I was.

'Aunty Barb, it's me! Guess where I am!'

'No idea m'duck,' she answered, using her favourite term of endearment that was a great Derbyshire phrase.

'I'm at Graceland, Barbie. I couldn't go in without ringing you!'

'O, you little bitch', she said fondly. 'Wish I was with you. When me and your dad...' She told me again about the trip and how great it was.

'Alright, Barbie, I've got to go on the tour. I will be thinking of you on the way around.' I was trying to end the call as Aunty Barb could chatter for hours when she got going. If I weren't careful I'd know who down the street had died, had accidents or given birth in the last month or two—people I had never known but that didn't matter to Barbie.

'OK, m'duck. Give my love to the King.' With that I left to follow in the footsteps of millions of other Elvis fans from all over the world.

Rach and I got on the small commercial bus that made the short drive across the road from the centre where you bought tickets and any kind of Elvis merchandise your heart should desire and through the famous gates to the house itself.

Off the bus, we duly marched behind other tourists all listening to the same audio-guided tour, which featured music by the man himself and commentary from those who knew him.

The Graceland mansion was much smaller than I expected, especially as Elvis was known for his extravagant gifts to others. And whilst the famous jungle room was slightly decadent, the rest of the house was surprisingly normal. I suppose for Elvis, having been born in a two-room home in Tupelo, Mississippi, this was indeed extravagant. It somehow made him more endearing to me.

I couldn't help but get tingles down the back of my neck as I listened to his classics whilst walking through the house he shared with Priscilla and Lisa Marie. And, after walking into his trophy building, I was surprised by just how many songs he had released and how many films... thirty-three! It is amazing that I recognised so many, given that when he died in 1977, I was just two years old. It goes to show how iconic the man is.

However, icon or not, he had a terrible sense of fashion. I don't care how attractive a man is, he shouldn't wear a white jumpsuit. It just isn't right! Admittedly, the originals are much better quality than the cheap copies I am used to seeing on friends at costume parties, but they are just as garish!

The last stop on the tour was the *Meditation Garden* where Elvis and members of his family were laid to rest. I'd forgotten that his twin brother, Jessie, had been stillborn and I couldn't help but wonder how that affected him growing up. Had knowing he was the one who survived somehow driven him to want to succeed more than the average person.

I have always found it interesting to understand the backgrounds of people who have been highly successful and found that many of them came from extremely poor, under-privileged pasts or had a history that was somehow marred by a traumatic event.

I thought about my own past, and realised that my formula for positive change had come out of a time when I felt most driven to get away and have a different life to the one I was living. The same feeling I had lying at the bottom of the stairs, which had been the catalyst for the changes I was now trying to create, and this trip.

Still in the implementation phase, I had a lot of dates to go and was still optimistic that I would find the love I was looking for, even though so far I had only really felt a connection with Sam.

In a reflective mood, after the tour, I couldn't resist buying Aunty Barb yet more Elvis trinkets. Graceland had lived up to my expectations, and the only thing I was disappointed by was the commerciality of it.

I wonder whether other fans like my Aunty, who loved Elvis so much despite never knowing him, felt the same slight twinge of pity for the man who, in death, seemed to have become just a business.

I tried to shrug off the thought and the melancholic state I had suddenly fallen into as Rach and I drove to B.B. King's Club on the famous Beale Street in Memphis, where I was supposed to be meeting my next date.

The club was known for its rhythm and blues, and such greats as Louis Armstrong, Muddy Waters and B.B. King had played there.

Date #8: Steven – You Missed Out On
Some Great Hickory-Smoked Ribs!

Whilst waiting for Steven to arrive, I read the menu and learnt that B.B. King's real name was Riley B. King. He got the moniker B.B. from his nickname when he started as the *Beale Street Blues Boy*.

After reading the menu at least four times and knowing exactly what I wanted to eat, I looked at my watch and saw that my date was twenty minutes late. I consumed a coke, ordered a second, and then rang him to see whether he was close. He didn't answer. I sent a text. After a few more minutes I got a short reply advising me that he was not coming.

In my younger days I would have obsessed about why he had stood me up. Had he seen me from outside and turned around? Had he met someone else but been too afraid to mention it? I could come up with scores of reasons for his behaviour that reflected me in a negative light rather than him and reduced my worth as a person because of my own insecurities. That was in my younger days.

After years of allowing other people to control my self-image and especially my ex-fiancé, Kyle, who had purposely decimated any belief I had in myself during our relationship purely for his own gain, I finally grew up.

Kyle had slowly but surely chipped away at my self-image throughout our relationship until I thought I was worthless – and was worried with all his lies that I was going slightly mad! His actions were driven by a need to control me and stop me from asking hard questions and realising he was playing me along whilst keeping his options open with his wife. I had always thought they were divorced but it turns out they were married during our entire relationship and, needless to say, she was the one he went back to when I had finally had enough and stood up for myself.

It was after this corrosive relationship had ended that Adam had come back to Australia to visit. Still reeling from the effects, when Adam had reached out I simply wasn't able to be there for him. I needed all my energy for myself to mend my heart and allow my open wounds time to heal.

So, as I sat there, I rationally decided that there could be tens of reasons for my date not showing and I was not to dwell on any of them. It wasn't my fault he was rude! I was here. I had done the right thing. That was all that mattered when it came to my being able to sleep peacefully in my bed at night.

I rang Rach and told her what had happened. She hadn't eaten yet so she joined me for some hickory-smoked ribs.

Hmm... ribs. Ribs are a meal not to be eaten on a first date as I learned when I was at university in the UK. I was all dressed up and wearing my best white shirt for my date with Jordan, who I had fancied for ages, only to drop a rib smothered in sauce down it within five minutes. I never got a second date... but at least he'd shown up for the first!!

Mississippi

There's a lot to do in Mississippi. Not surprisingly, you can cruise down the Mississippi, which flows through thirty-one other states, from Minnesota to the Mississippi River Delta at the Gulf of Mexico.

The state is also great for history buffs like my dad as it was the place of many Civil War battles.

But, I didn't want to do either of these things. I wanted to visit the museum where in 1894 the first Coca-Cola was bottled.

To my parents chagrin, I have been addicted to Coca-Cola since I was a kid and was super excited to visit this sacred site in Vicksburg.

Date #9: Richard – I Need A Coke Hit!

My date, Richard, though having lived nearby all of his life, had never been to the Biedenharn Coca-Cola Museum, and it turned out he prefers Pepsi... I should have known that the date was doomed as soon as he told me this when we met outside!

Still we went in. As we walked around, looking at a variety of exhibits and equipment that was used for the first bottling process, I found myself talking quite a lot. Richard, on the other hand, didn't seem to be listening, taking in any of the information on the tour or participating in any way.

I began to wonder what I could do to get his interest, when I mentioned that I planned to do some kayaking in Mexico at the end of my trip but had forgotten to get insurance to cover it. His eyes lit up. I thought it was because he liked kayaking, but it was because he loved insurance!

I must have unconsciously made the link with insurance to have been talking of it in the first place, but not having read his profile in a while, I'd forgotten it was what he did for a living. He proceeded to share with me all sorts of nuggets on policies and the companies I could talk to. I now felt like I imagine he had at the start of the date. After just over an hour together, I was more than a little grateful when he had to return to the job he clearly loved so much.

Meanwhile I popped back into the museum for a coke float to get a much-needed hit of caffeine to wake me back up. I don't often wonder what the other person thinks after a date with me, unless I really like him, and then I will obsess for hours about it. But sipping on my coke float, I did wonder whether Richard had found me as intensely boring as I'd found him.

Isn't it strange how many different people there are in the world with all their peculiar likes and dislikes? So far, apart from Sam, I hadn't felt a special connection with any of my dates.

I spoke to Rachael about it in the car as she drove us onwards to Louisiana.

'You know Rach, this dating game is actually much harder than I anticipated.' I said as I twisted in my seat to get a better view of her as she was concentrating on the road.

'After all of the nightmare dates you've been on this trip, I have to admit I'm glad I'm happily married and out of the dating scene,' she said with a grin glancing across at me. 'It's been funny from my end to hear all of your stories afterwards, but why are you doing this to yourself?'

I squirmed slightly, both inwardly and as I rummaged in the back pocket of my jeans to extricate my wallet and pull out the list of goals that were safely ensconced within.

'It's because I want to find a partner', I quoted.

'Yes, but, why?'

'I'm lonely, Rach. I've been single now for pretty much six years. And before you remind me, I'm not counting Clark! Both you and I know I never trusted him, knowing he'd cheated on his last girlfriend for years.'

'Do you reckon you can ever trust anyone?' Rachael probed. 'I'm getting to know your track history of dating and even before this journey you haven't exactly had a good run of it. From everything you've said, Adam was the only one you really trusted and even he didn't manage to get things quite right.'

My pulse quickened and palms started to sweat as I reacted with panic at what she had just said. She was right, of course. All of my relationships had only served to reinforce my long held belief that the only person you can truly rely on in this world is yourself. Yet, I so desperately hoped that someone out there would prove me wrong.

'God, I hope so,' I responded. 'It's easy to meet people to chat to for a few hours, but finding someone to spend the rest of my life with is a whole different ball game. Each person I've met does have something unique to say. And from an objective standpoint, I am finding it interesting that everyone shares one thing in common: We all seem to yearn for a connection with others and a person to love us.'

'A bit deep for you Mel!' Rachael quipped, trying to use humour to break my suddenly solemn mood.

'I know. I'm doomed to a life of singledom!' I replied trying to joke about a reality that I had real concerns I was destined for.

'But seriously, you managed to find the right guy, Rach. Simon is fabulous. How did you do it?'

Rachael's lips pursed into a wry smile and darting a look in my direction she said, 'Just luck... and timing. I had let go of my past demons and was ready.

'I'm not saying it's easy Mel, but there are some good men out there who are loyal and trustworthy. And whilst I don't envy you all your dates, I admire you for having the guts to go on them. You are certainly giving yourself the best chance of finding the needle in the haystack and meeting the man who you feel you can really trust. Keep going, if he's out there... you'll find him.'

I sat back, taking a deep breath and letting her words sink in. 'You're right.' I replied feeling more grounded now. 'And on the bright side...' I rallied, seeing the positive again in having all of these dates, '...while I'm searching, my networking skills are being so finely honed that I am never going to have a problem walking into a room full of strangers and making small talk again!'

She let out a loud laugh. 'That's true! God help us, there'll be no stopping you when you eventually get back to Canberra... you'll be the networking Queen!'

We drove on – the party atmosphere of New Orleans beckoned.

CHAPTER 6

Tenacity

s Rachael continued along the highway, I fell silent, thinking about what we had talked about. I was now having nightly conversations with Sam and was finding that, the longer I was away, the greater the pull was to see him again.

A big part of me wanted to convince Rachael that going to New Orleans was a bad idea, and that, instead, we should go back and enjoy the California sunshine in San Diego.

I also wanted her to meet Sam and give me her assessment. They had already spoken on the phone once or twice when she'd answered while I was driving, and she said she liked the little she knew of him.

Two things prevented me from turning around.

The first and most important was a part of my Positive Change Formula: the fifth step, Tenacity.

To me tenacity means seeing things through to the end no matter what curveballs life throws at you. It meant that, whether I was falling for Sam, broke my leg or got offered a million-dollar job, I could not give in and should not go back. I had to, and wanted to, fulfil my plan of dating fifty men in fifty states.

The second reason was Rachael.

She was flying back to Australia from Orlando, Florida, so we were committed to continue on our voyage east. She was also really looking forward to New Orleans and our spending some time together there and in Florida as we were getting to the stage of the trip where I had scheduled fewer dates and would have more free time.

Thelma and Louise stuck together and so would Rachael and I!

I looked over at Rach. Her long dark hair had fallen slightly over her face and her eyes were busy scanning the road ahead for traffic... and traffic police.

We had more in common than either of us had realised, which was probably why we were drawn to each other and got along so well.

We had agreed that whether I found Mr. Right or not, together with her husband, Simon, at some point, we would return to the Grand Canyon and do the two-day walk to the bottom and back.

But for now we had a night in New Orleans to look forward to.

Louisiana

In New Orleans the hotel booking website had come up trumps once again. Our hotel was just around the corner from Bourbon Street so, even though it was after 10 p.m., we headed that way in search of food.

We'd decided the next night would be our big night out, so we just wandered up and down the street looking for a restaurant. After a couple of laps, a bouncer came to our aid, pointing us in the direction of a good restaurant that would still be serving this late. In return we promised to pop back and have a quick drink.

Being the good girls that we are, we dutifully returned with the idea that we'd have one drink before bed. However, when we entered the bar, a band was playing '80s and '90s rock. Rachael and I grinned at each other, and our quick-drink plan went out the window.

The music emanating loudly from the stage was that of our teens, and I was reminded of my favourite drink from those years: Jack Daniels and coke. I ordered doubles for us both.

Hours later, one drink had turned into ten as Rach and I were being bombarded with free shots from staff and punters alike, who were thoroughly enjoying watching us bust a move on the dance floor. I am no Ginger Rogers, but when it comes to rock music, I can head-bang and play air guitar with the best of them... and it turns out Rach can too!

We boogied the night away genuinely enjoying ourselves and reliving our glory days.

Our happiness must have been infectious because, in addition to buying us drinks, people joined us on the floor. Even the band got involved, singling us out for a special mention.

The band later got involved in other ways too—well, the drummer anyway!

Date #10: Max – Music And Magic In New Orleans

I'd noticed him because he didn't really look like he fit in with the rest of the band. He was too clean cut and gentlemanly looking for his surroundings. I wondered why he was there.

Every time I looked at him, he was also looking at me, so I flashed him an occasional smile. This was enough to lure him over during one of their breaks. Jack Daniels in hand for me and Rach—he'd obviously found out from the bar staff what we were drinking—he made his approach.

As I had suspected, he didn't fit what I thought of as the stereotypical mould for a drummer in New Orleans... or anywhere for that matter. After talking to him for a short time he pulled out a piece of paper and started tearing it into pieces. Someone once told me that when people fiddle with and tear up beer bottle labels and beer mats it is a sign of sexual tension. I unconsciously stepped back a little.

When he finished ripping the paper, he opened it up to produce two squares linked together. I looked at it open- mouthed.

'I'm impressed,' I said. 'How did you do it?'

He started talking about math and physics and other subjects about which I am completely ignorant. I looked at him blankly.

'Where did you go to university?' I asked.

Having been to seven universities, this is a subject I understand. I always joke I got thrown out of six, but actually I just love learning and needed to convert my qualifications when I was in Australia, and then decided to continue on to do a Masters.

He told me he studied at Stanford University and not surprisingly majored in physics. We continued to chat and he returned to subject areas that I knew little about, but he gave me the impression that not only was he smart but he was super smart. He was also funny, observant and sweet.

So, when he asked us to stay until the end of the next set, how could I refuse? Rachael and I were having too much fun anyway.

A little after 3 a.m. (I think) the place began to wind down and Max, the drummer, finally finished work. He tried to convince Rach and me to head to another club, but we were now exhausted.

Rach was happy for me to go it alone but no matter how sweet Max appeared, he was very much sober and I wasn't. That could prove a recipe for disaster and I'd enjoyed the night so much I didn't want anything to tarnish it now.

I'd learnt from bitter experience not to go it alone and separate from friends after a night out. A couple of mine had left me in a very awkward and potentially dangerous situation one night thinking they were doing the right thing since they believed I was keen on a guy that we had met. In actual fact, I was just being polite.

When I had looked round and not found them anywhere, I was left stranded in a town I didn't know very well and unsure of the exact address to go back to. I called and called them, but they were probably at another club and didn't hear the phone. In any case, they didn't respond.

I had been lucky that the guy was a good bloke and understood my predicament. He offered me a place to stay without any strings attached, but it could so easily have turned into a nightmare scenario. I never wanted to be in that situation again and made it a rule never ever to leave a friend behind or get separated from the group.

With Max though, we did let him drive us back to the hotel and I agreed to a date with him the next evening. When we stopped at the hotel, Rachael discreetly stepped outside to allow him to give me a kiss goodnight.

I hopped out a minute later and Rach and I set off only to find Max reversing quickly to tell us that we were heading in the wrong direction. He pointed across the street so we could clearly see we were actually standing right across the road from our hotel... oops!

I woke up what felt like only a couple of hours later, with a raging hangover. I looked at my watch, it was 11 a.m. I was supposed to have a lunch date with a guy called Eric at 1 p.m. but couldn't face it. I'm not proud to admit that I rang Eric and asked if he wouldn't mind if I cancelled our date. I told him the truth, that I was seriously hung over and not in a fit state to meet anyone.

'Seriously, Eric, I am so sorry.' I said apologetically.

'It's OK, Mel,' he replied kindly. 'It would have been nice to meet you, but I understand.'

He was so sweet about it, I felt more than a little guilty for standing him up. But, I also needed time to get over the effects of the hangover and spend some quality time with Rach before meeting Max later, as I had now promised to do. There is only so much a girl can cram into one day. I promised if I came back through he would be the first person I called and hung up, relieved.

I squinted bleary-eyed at Rachael, who looked as though she felt just as bad as I did, and we decided it was an absolute necessity to find a greasy spoon that served fry-ups—the known hangover cure.

A fry-up for me normally consists of bacon, eggs, baked beans, fried toast and fried tomato, and it is a requirement after a big night out. It always makes me feel better and I have devised my own theory that it serves to soak up the remnants of alcohol in the system. True or not I have no idea, but it works for me!

Not finding quite what we were looking for, we settled for a diner where we at least got eggs and I decided now was the time to try grits as well.

Grits, New Orleans style (not sure if there is any other), was the consistency of runny egg whites before they're cooked and looked like soggy rice. The taste and consistency reminded me of the scene from the *Matrix* when Neo eats his first meal on the Nebuchadnezzar and finds it looks horrible and tastes of nothing.

I didn't understand the appeal. I asked the waiter's advice. He told me many people add something for flavour. I gave it a go. I added salt to part of it. No good. I added sugar to another portion. Still nothing. I added maple syrup. Nope. I gave up. I still don't understand why people like grits, but at least I tried!

Feeling slightly more human after downing a couple of rounds of toast and eggs, Rachael and I now had most of the day together, so we decided a quiet cruise along the Mississippi was just what the doctor ordered.

I'm not sure that one is supposed to sleep on a Mississippi river cruise, but it's pretty comfortable if you manage to get a seat early enough and stay in the shade. We woke up about an hour in and had a steady meander around the ship, amused to find that the two engines powering us were called Thelma and Louise.

Back on shore we continued with the theme of the day—trying Southern style hospitality (food) and tucked into a Po' boy.

This does have some taste but is basically meat drenched in sauce on a baguette. I didn't like it. Neither did Rachael. Ah well, I felt sure if I introduced the locals here to the English chip buttie (a big bread roll lathered in butter and crammed with thick french fries topped off with gravy, baked beans or mushy peas depending on your personal taste) they may not like it either.

With our tummies full again, Rach and I decided it was time to retreat to the hotel for another nap. As Max had to work, we were meeting for an early evening drink. I woke to a text advising me that he'd arrived at the bar and was waiting. Oops! I hurriedly gave myself a quick sink wash before getting dressed and heading out.

Max continued to impress me with his unique insight into the world. The fact that, with all of his brains, he chose to be a professional musician over earning serious money in a conventional career only made me like him more. He was following his passion and happy doing something he loved.

In that respect he reminded me of Adam, who had followed his dreams instead of settling for a conventional life. It was one of the things I most admired about Adam and one of the things that drove me the most nuts. Yet, when I thought about it, maybe his example was a big part of the impetus for my trip.

The one thing that made Adam's death more bearable was that he had lived the life he wanted. When you looked at the places he had been and the lives he had touched, you couldn't help but see that he had squeezed more into his thirty-seven years on the planet than most people who live into their eighties.

He didn't just see a country, he really lived in it. All around Asia he had stayed with the locals and taken part in their daily lives. By the time he left a place, he really felt it in his bones rather than only having a superficial understanding as most of the travellers do who just pass through.

Maybe this trip was my version of how Adam travelled. Maybe I was trying to recreate that understanding of a place and its people through dating strangers.

And, it was working. Before this trip my view of Americans was that they were loud, brash, chewed gum with their mouths open, and believed the rest of the world (if they realised there was a world outside the US of A) couldn't possibly survive without them.

Now I saw them in a very different light. The majority of the people I had met on my travels had been warm and welcoming. They were generous and seemed genuinely concerned for the welfare of others. And, most of those I had spoken to were now very aware of the general negative impression many international travellers had of them and were working hard to change it.

There were good people and bad all over the world. Some people met the stereotype and some didn't. Hating being labelled or automatically judged for my looks, sex or heritage by others, I realised I had been just as guilty of this action. And I was incorrect and unfair in doing so. As ever, travel reminded me of my prejudices and how wrong they were. I smiled at this realisation.

I'll never know if Adam had an idea that he wouldn't be here for long and needed to make the most out of every minute, but he certainly did so. He was an inspiration and I cannot help but believe he was proud of me for following his example.

After my date with Max, I sat down and wrote to Adam before going to sleep.

Hey Adamski,

I met a guy here I think you'd like. He reminded me of you.

So many people and places still remind me of you, Adamski. I suppose that will always be the case.

But, I'm feeling more ready to just hold onto the happy memories of our relationship rather than the pain and regret of losing you.

What do you think, perhaps I am ready to move on?

God, I wish I could talk to you though. I miss your voice. I miss our chats and sharing my thoughts and feelings with you.

Writing to you isn't the same as your laughing, cajoling or calming me about something that in the grand scheme of things isn't that important.

This trip is causing me to rethink what's important and what isn't.

I suppose I should have learnt that lesson when you passed away. I guess I always knew that it was our relationships with people that are the most important rather than work, material things or holidays.

It's just hard to break old habits.

Although in the end I became a slave to work and it used me rather than the other way around, it really did help me take my mind off of losing you until I was ready to deal with it. I guess my brain was processing it in the background the whole time because, if it wasn't, there is no way I would have been ready to do this trip and really embrace the idea of finding a new love.

Will I find one, Adam? Have I already met him? I don't think it's Max although I really like and admire him. I just don't feel the connection I did and still do with Sam.

I have to admit part of me hopes that Sam is the guy for me. I don't know why, but I think I'm falling for him.

Rachael made a comment this morning that whenever I speak to Sam my eyes light up and I'm always happy afterwards. Not like me at all to let a man have such an impact.

I'm not sure that I'm comfortable with it to be honest. I'm not sure if I want to put my heart on the line again. I don't know if I can take losing someone again if it doesn't work out.

O well Adamski. In for a penny, in for a pound.

Night x

The trip to New Orleans was not quite what I'd planned but that didn't matter... it had turned out much better, and I had a new friend in Max, who I had a feeling I'd stay in touch with.

Alabama
Date #11: Adrian - Safety First

My next date Adrian, who lived in Mobile, Alabama, had called when I was hung over and I'd stupidly agreed he could pick me up at the hotel.

I am usually really careful about giving away where I live to men I don't know well and the experience with Nathan in New Mexico had reminded me of why. However, by the time I realised my mistake, I felt obliged to go along with the plan. Convention and manners can lead you to do stupid things sometimes.

Whilst driving to Mobile, I was kicking myself for getting into what could be a dangerous situation. As Rach slept, I quietly fumed and cursed myself. Why had I agreed? Why didn't I have the nerve to tell him I wanted to meet at the restaurant?

The situation and my discomfort reminded me of another time in my life when I believed I'd let myself down—when I had been date raped.

For years, I silently punished myself for what happened that day when I was sixteen. And until I went to grief counselling after Adam died and that trauma came out as well, I had never told anyone everything that happened.

I was so ashamed of the incident that I thought everyone knew simply by looking at me. I remember getting home afterwards and showering and scrubbing myself, trying to feel clean.

I've run through the scenario so many times, trying to work out what I'd done to cause it, why I didn't stop it. At one point, years later, I even managed to convince myself it had been consensual, although I knew the truth in my heart.

When it came up during the grief counselling, I finally acknowledged what had been eating me up for almost twenty years. I hated myself for being so weak and didn't feel worthy of being loved by anyone.

What I struggled with most was not the actual rape, but my reaction to it at the time. I'm strong. I always have been. I'm known for my resilience. I'm a survivor. Knock me down and I always get up swinging. It's my personality. So why on that occasion didn't I respond that way? I couldn't understand nor forgive myself for not reacting at a time when I needed to the most.

The counsellor asked specific questions about how my body had reacted at the time. I remembered struggling and then asking the guy to stop and, when he didn't, I had an almost outer-body experience where my brain was watching what was happening whilst my body just lay there and went completely limp.

I explained to the counsellor that I'd never been able to make sense of my actions that night. Why? Why did I freeze? Why did I let it happen? Why do I hate myself rather than the guy who did it?

She then explained the different mechanisms the brain uses for survival. Apparently, research has identified several although there are still discussions around terminology. She listed five: friend, fight, flight, freeze and flop, the last having been added just a couple of years ago she told me.

These reactions are apparently instinctive and result from signals given by a part of the brain called the amygdala when a threat is detected.

The brain has three sections: the lower, middle limbic and upper brain. In times of trauma, the upper brain stops working and allows the instinctive survival mechanisms of the lower and middle brain to kick in. Apparently the reason for this is that the brain prioritises survival in times of great stress.

When the counsellor analysed what had occurred with me, it was clear my first reaction was to 'fight', followed by trying to 'friend' the guy, by asking him to stop, before moving into the final two reactions of 'freeze' and 'flop'.

Apparently, humans do in times of great stress what other animals do when hunted—they will either run or freeze. And for animals, if freezing does not work and they get caught, their last resort is to go limp and pretend to be dead because many predators won't eat meat that has already been killed.

I remember arguing that I was not an animal and I've always reacted to threats by standing my ground and fighting.

She told me that whilst that may be the case in other scenarios, my upper brain had obviously shut down because of the stress, and my lower and middle brain had kicked in and reacted differently.

This sounded like a good explanation, but I wanted further proof if I was going to be able to rationalise it after so many years. So I did a ton of reading around the subject and it appeared to be true.

In reading up on the subject again recently, I was impressed to see that in 2010 there was more written research released by a sexualised trauma specialist in the UK, named Zoe Lodrick.

She explained the flop phenomenon some more and talked about the fact that unfortunately these days, the instinctive reactions don't actually help. But, because they're hard wired into our systems at a very basic level, sometimes they can't be overridden. Equally unfortunately, she states that this reaction can be perceived as acquiescence to an action when it's not.

All over again, I felt a sense of relief as I took in what she had written. So, I was not alone in responding as I did to this event.

I read on and saw that she said, in the short-term, this reaction helps the brain to cope with what's happening, but unfortunately when the higher brain functions kick in this may no longer be the case.

This was my situation when the rape was over. My normal reactions returned, and I couldn't make sense of why I'd not just fought like hell, scratched his eyes out, kicked him in the balls and got the hell out of there.

I wish I'd known this earlier and that I'd gotten help before. If this had been explained to me two decades ago maybe then I wouldn't have spent the better part of my life blaming myself and unconsciously destroying my relationships because I couldn't cope with trust or intimacy.

However, maybe even if someone had explained to me why I had responded the way I did back when I was sixteen, I still would not have been mature enough to forgive myself for such a huge mistake, even though it was an instinctive reaction. Understanding and forgiveness of others and, more specifically myself, has come with age.

Although the conscious thinking part of me still believes I could have belted the living shit out of the guy if I'd used the adrenaline rush I normally get in times of stress, who knows if this reaction would have caused a worse result for me in the end.

After going over all of this in my head yet again as I tore up the freeway, I reminded myself just how strong I actually am and how far I've come. To hell with being polite—my safety is more important.

When I saw an exit, I pulled off and then found a safe place to pull over. I got the mobile out and called Adrian and advised him of a change of plans. I would meet him at the restaurant.

He wasn't at all upset or put out. When I met him later, he turned out to be a perfectly lovely gentleman, and we had a great few hours together.

I know a large part of this was because I was now more relaxed, confident and happier with myself because I'd taken control of the situation rather than because of anything Adrian did or didn't do. And, to be honest, although I didn't think I would see Adrian again, I did leave the date feeling good about myself and, hell, that can't be bad.

Florida

Date #12: Mark – Three's A Crowd, Leave Your Smart Phone At Home

My date in Florida was with Mark from Miami. Coming from Alabama, it was a hell of a long way to drive, but Rachael and I were ahead of schedule and she was up for a couple of days chilling out on a beach and taking in the sunshine, so we decided to go for it.

Mark seemed smart, witty and kind in his profile, but the main reason I said yes to the date was because he was seriously cute. In all of his photos, Mark had a mischievous look in his eye and a wide grin that could create a smile on even the most miserable person's face.

He was also just my 'type'. I always seem to be particularly attracted to men who are broad and muscular with dark hair and darker features. Maybe it's because I have such pale English skin that I'm attracted to the opposite.

When I got to the beachside restaurant where we were meeting for breakfast I was early, which gave me time to nip to the bathroom and pour some water over myself to cool down. Even at 8 a.m. it was hot and humid.

The heat and my nerves at meeting this particular date had combined to make me a big red blob. I sloshed water over my face, held my wrists under the cold tap and even took the drastic measure of going into the stalls and stripping down to my underwear in an effort to cool myself down quicker.

I only looked slightly better when I got out of the bathroom and settled into my seat. However, even looking like a big red blob, I was obviously recognisable to Mark, who turned up a few minutes later. Unfortunately, I cannot say the same for him.

If he hadn't come up and introduced himself, I would not have known he was my date. He looked nothing like his photos.

Why do people do that? Are they really so insecure that, on dating websites, they need to put up photos of someone else or of themselves twenty years ago? I am sure it can't help in the long run.

Although bitterly disappointed and very surprised, I tried not to let it show. If there is one thing I've learnt so far on this trip, it's not to judge a book by its cover. I hid my surprise quickly, smiled warmly, and started chatting to Mark.

He made this difficult by checking his smart phone every two minutes because, apparently, he had a big meeting and very little time to prepare, plus some deals 'were going down'. I began to feel like a spare part on the date, and Mark gave me the distinct impression he would prefer to be on his own with his phone.

After that awkward breakfast, Mark made excuses to leave, and then claimed he'd forgotten to bring his wallet, leaving me with the bill. I felt, I am sure, like many men do when women do this—used, angry and annoyed.

In speaking to Rachael about it as we laid on the beach afterwards we decided it was time that I stopped going for the same 'type'. Rach very insightfully suggested that if my usual type worked, I wouldn't still be single, so maybe I should branch out.

I realised that if I'd seen Sam or Max on one of the internet dating sites I was using, I never would have chosen them as a date. I would have classed Sam as too short and Max as too chubby simply because he didn't have obvious arm and chest muscles. Yet they were the only two men I really liked so far. Time to change things up a bit!

For now, though, I had four days left with Rachael. She'd been so wonderful during my dates—sightseeing, sunbathing or reading on her own, many times even having lunch, dinner or sometimes breakfast by herself—that I wanted to spend the last few days, just the two of us, checking out Florida.

On our penultimate day together, as we made our way to Orlando, we headed to Kennedy Space Centre and spent hours gawking at the amazing engineering feats the staff at NASA have achieved over the years in getting mankind to outer space and the moon.

I remember visiting Kennedy Space Centre with my family when I was about eight years old. As we took the tour memories came flooding back and I remembered having been able to get much closer to the action because there was a lot less security—no need to present passports to gain entrance and be ferried about in tightly guarded and organised groups during the tours.

As a child I had been fascinated to learn more about outer space and I had even added astronaut to my list of future occupations, which already included prime minister and lawyer. It was struck from the list at age eleven after the shuttle Challenger exploded, killing all seven astronauts onboard. I remember thinking that law and politics were much less dangerous... little did I know.

Almost twenty years later, that day with Rachael at Kennedy Space Centre reignited the spark of interest and wonder I had felt as a child. It's so easy to forget just how amazing the world and the universe are, not to mention the great human accomplishments of the last century. I was reminded of a JFK quote, 'One person can make a difference and everyone should try.'

As Rach and I rested over a lunch of burger and fries in one of the diners they have at the Centre, I spoke to her about another of the goals I wanted to achieve in the next year – to change careers.

In discussing what motivates each of us unsurprisingly, seeing as we had both been drawn to the Government, a desire to serve the community was high on our lists.

And, for me, after my eyes had been opened to the plight of the girls in Nepal, I felt a drive to support underprivileged women and help arm them with the education they needed to be able to have a choice in where and how they lived.

As always when I spoke of the issue my voice started to rise, and, as I thumped my burger back down on the plate, I said passionately, 'You know Rach, I would love to be able to build a whole school for those girls, not just support one or two of them. That would really give me a sense of fulfilment!'

'Well, it would certainly be different from what you have been doing for the last couple of years', Rach noted drily as she picked up a couple of fries. She looked at me, and after a pause said, 'Lining the pockets of a large corporation.'

I wanted to argue with her, but I couldn't. Although I had felt I was serving a purpose whilst working for the Government, I had indeed lost that feeling when I moved to the private sector.

'Well, whatever I do next', I said with confidence, 'it seems clear now that it needs to be in the service and support of others. I don't have a specific job in mind, but at least knowing that narrows the field.'

I dipped my fries in some ketchup and added, 'And, even though I am only part way through this journey, I know one other thing for sure. My purpose is not attached to being someone's partner or wife. I want to find a man, Rach, but whether I find him or not, it doesn't change who I am. And it certainly doesn't define me.'

'Now, *that* is the Mel I know' Rach said, beaming at me across the table. 'Welcome back!'

Kennedy Space Centre was a fitting end to the road trip Rachael and I enjoyed together. Although it wasn't quite the re-enactment of Thelma and Louise, it was close enough.

We'd—rather I'd—met lots of guys along the way (just not Brad Pitt), and we'd gone over the edge of the Grand Canyon (only a little way and on foot, not, thank goodness, to a fiery death in a car) and, I'm ashamed to say, we'd been ticketed by the cops three times for speeding (but thankfully neither of us had been locked up). All in all, I think we did a damn fine job.

The next morning, as I watched Rachael's, confident, long-legged stride into Orlando's airport terminal, I realised just how much I'd miss her. Her cheerful smile and happy brown eyes had buoyed me. And when I drove away and saw one of her long brown hairs on the back of the car seat, I felt sad.

I realised that whilst men are all very well and it's great to have a wonderful partner, it shouldn't be all or nothing.

Friends can provide a balance and perspective that partners may not. I definitely wanted both in my life and was so grateful that despite my being quieter and more distant in the past few years, I still had many wonderful, supportive friends.

Georgia

Date #13: Phil – Art And Truck-Driving

I wound the window down and cranked up the radio. 'It's just you and me now, Randy,' I said to my trusty GPS. 'I know you can get cranky but don't go misbehaving and leading me astray now will you? We've got a lot of miles to go together, so just play nice.' I cajoled as we headed north to Georgia and my date there with a gentleman by the name of Phil.

Phil knew a thing or two about long-distance driving as he was a truck driver and had covered every state in the US several times over. We'd organised to meet just over the state line at a small Italian restaurant he knew about.

He had given me the address to plug into the GPS and I could see from the screen that I was going to make our date with plenty of time to spare. I eased off the gas, took a deep cleansing breath and smiled. On the road again!

I arrived early at the Italian restaurant Phil had directed me to, and so had he. I recognised him straight away although at six-foot five he was taller than I anticipated. Whilst stocky, he wasn't overweight and his head was shaved completely clean. He had a New York drawl and he proudly told me, an Italian heritage.

As our table wasn't ready, we shared a bottle of white wine and settled in at the bar.

'Well, Melanie', he said, addressing me politely, 'It sounds like you are on quite an adventure.'

'You could say that. And it's really only just begun.' I smiled. 'I've made the trip from west to east but now I'm heading back again.'

When I told him about the long solo drive west I would soon undertake he gave me some tips on how to stay awake—lots of coffee, regular stops, loud music and open windows.

To keep himself entertained whilst out on the road, he told me, he had developed a keen interest in photography.

In fact, he said, opening up a bag he had with him 'I've brought some of my photos to show you if you're interested'.

He clearly had a passion for photography and as I flipped through the stills of everyday objects, people and situations I was impressed by his ability to make the mundane seem almost enigmatic. Some of his photos were really good, and I enjoyed listening to him talk about life on the road as I sifted through them.

I admit to having preconceived notions when I saw that Phil was a truck driver. So talking about photography and art was the last thing I had expected on our date.

I was again pleasantly surprised at the strangeness of life—although I do think it odd to bring a photo album to a first date. If I'd not been interested, it could've been a big mistake, which, Phil admitted, it was on a few of his previous dates. He told me the ladies had just flipped through a couple of pages, and then shut the album. I wondered why he continued to bring it and pondered the possibility it was a test.

He seemed grateful that I actually spent the time to go through the entire album and appeared interested in him and his views as I asked him questions along the way. I think just because of that, he asked me out on a second date.

'If we're in the same state at the same time in the next few months I'd love to have dinner again,' I said. 'I may even share with you the photos of all the places I've been!' I laughed as we parted company.

As I walked back to my rental car, I thought back on my dates so far. Although several had been what I could term strange, it had been wonderful to meet them all and hear their unique perspectives on life. None of them though had come close to making me feel as I did with Sam.

It may not have helped that Sam and I were still chatting every night by phone, but I really don't think that would have made a difference to my wanting to see any of the guys again or not. It really hit me between the eyes that Sam was special and someone I wanted to spend more time with.

My original plan from Georgia was to head back to the western states to attend two conferences in Nevada. I'd signed up for another

Loral Langemeier event and was also going to catch up with my friend and coach, Kevin, in Las Vegas.

I'd known Kevin since I was in the Army back in 2001, where I had worked for him briefly. We had become good friends and over time he and his wife, Barb, had become like another set of surrogate parents. I had a habit of people adopting me as an extra daughter, and he and Barb, together with Daisy and Andrew who were looking after my dog, Jessie, were the parents I turned to for advice when I was at home in Australia.

Kevin, as a professional coach, had always helped me clarify what it was I wanted next out of my career when I got restless—which was generally every eighteen months.

The last time I had seen him had been in July in the middle of the Australian winter. Knowing about my trip, we'd organised to have lunch together before I left. Although it was a bright clear day, the temperatures were hovering around freezing when we'd met up in a Canberra cafe.

As we'd been talking about my trip he told me about his too. He and Barb were also US bound and coming to the country to attend an international coaching conference. We agreed tentatively to meet up and then he'd leaned over and said to me 'You know what, Mel. You should come to the conference too.'

'Really? Why?' I'd asked, cautiously wrapping my fingers around the hot chocolate I was drinking in an effort to get warm.

'Because I have an inkling you'd like it... and the people' he'd replied. 'You have all the skill sets it takes to become a great coach'.

I'd read up about the conference after we talked and decided, *what the hell.* The speakers they had lined up over the three days were impressive and it didn't hurt to find out more. So, I signed up.

As I sat in the parking lot suddenly uncertain of what I wanted to do next it would have been good to have been able to pick the phone up and speak to Kevin now.

I was meant to drive through a new set of states and have more dates before reaching Vegas but I got a knot in my stomach as I thought about it. Instead of plugging in the coordinates for my hotel, I unconsciously plugged in San Diego. Quickly Randy had flashed up an approximate driving time of almost forty hours. I blinked as I registered what I had done. Driving forty hours back to San Diego—that was a crazy idea.

Still, I got out of the car and rummaged in the back until I found the information on the coaching conference. I checked the date, did a rough calculation of how long it had taken Rachael and I to drive across country and to meet up with someone in each state.

Then, I took out my list of goals again from my wallet and ran through it.

Find a partner was my number one goal.

I looked again at Randy's screen glowing in the darkness. Almost forty hours of straight driving to San Diego.

'Sod it' I muttered and hit the road. I was heading back to see Sam.

CHAPTER 7

Integrity

*D*espite returning to San Diego sooner than I had planned, I assured myself that I would continue with my dates in the other states.

I determined to keep travelling after catching up quickly with Sam before the two conferences. I knew that if, when I saw him again, we decided to have a relationship, I would be sorely tempted to stop.

In my formula I was at step six, Integrity.

By its very nature, implementation is the longest phase of positive change, and without steps five and six, tenacity and integrity, the change would stop all together and victory would remain elusive.

That isn't to say that a plan cannot be adapted, there is always room for improvisation as not everything can be planned for in advance. Sometimes reality gets in the way and for a while the plan may need to be put on the back burner, as long as the goal is not forgotten and the plan is re-initiated as soon as possible there is no issue with this. The integrity refers to remaining true to the longer term goal that was set.

Sam was a test of my integrity to be true to myself and my goals. If my goals had remained exactly the same as when I had written them, then I would have some flexibility, as my goal was to meet my life partner, not date fifty guys in fifty states.

However, that plan changed at the Fast Cash conference. I had now made a commitment to write a book about my fifty dates.

I had to demonstrate integrity not only to myself, but to the people who had the faith in me to buy a book about my travels... before I had even completed them.

Besides, if I hadn't gone to the conference and made that commitment, Sam's friend would never have introduced us in the first place.

That settled it. No matter what happened with Sam, California was only going to be a quick interlude, and that was final!

California, again... and Nevada!

Shortly after setting off in the direction of California, I realised I was still very much in the deep south as the only channels that seemed to be available were Christian radio. After listening to one too many songs about God, I thanked Him (or Her) when my mobile rang and it was Sam.

'I thought you'd be lonely without Rachael,' he said.

'So I wanted to check in.'

'Was it only this morning I dropped her off? It's been a long day.'

'Are you at a hotel for the night yet? I wanted to make sure you had arrived safely after your date. I'm a bit worried about you driving all by yourself now.'

His concern touched me, even as I said casually, 'The date's over and I'm back on the highway. I've decided to push through for a couple of hours. I'm feeling wide awake, so no need to stress.'

We talked a bit about our respective day. Sam was about to start a new contract on a construction site, where he would be working on the 2-10 p.m. shift and was enjoying his last two days of freedom. He'd just got back from the boxing club, where he trained several times a week, and admitted that he had a black eye that was now on the mend.

I didn't tell him that I might see him before his eye had completely healed. He was concerned enough about my driving on my own I felt no need to worry him further by telling him I was driving straight there. Plus, given I had to stop to sleep, eat, and take breaks etc, I wasn't sure how long it would actually take me.

But, the real reason I didn't say anything was because I wanted to surprise him. I just hoped it would be a pleasant surprise.

I admit I pushed more than I should have. The drive back was mammoth! I was supposed to stop every few hours, but I regularly pushed on for seven hours at a time, only stopping when I was beginning to fall asleep and needed gas and caffeine. Since I rarely drink coffee, the large cup sizes in US gas stations definitely kept me going.

Unfortunately, it also gave me the shakes and, when I did stop for the night, I found I couldn't actually sleep. I was so wired that on the two nights I pulled over, I only stayed five hours in each hotel. It was almost impossible to sleep or relax.

On the morning of the second full day of driving, I started out at 5 a.m. and cleared the Texan state border thirty minutes later. I carried on through Tucson and thought of Diego. I wondered how he was doing with his allergies, but there was no way I was going to stop and find out.

An hour later I found myself stuck in early morning rush hour traffic in Phoenix. Slowly I made my way through it and out the other side, breathing a huge sigh of relief as I got back on the open highway on the turn off to California and San Diego.

I was happily humming along to the radio and imagining Sam's face when suddenly, a flatbed truck ahead of me, carrying large metal sheds starting *shedding* its load.

There was no warning as the first shed began to fall. Adrenaline kicked in as I veered left narrowly missing it as it hit the tarmac and bounced to the right side of the motorway.

I put my foot down on the gas and kept as wide a berth as I could as I tried to get past and out of danger's way. When I was past, I looked in the rear view mirror and saw another shed, toppling off the side.

Heart racing, I realised I was breathing fast and consciously slowed it down and focussed again on what was in front rather than behind me.

'That was close, Meg. Your guardian angel is working overtime again,' I told myself.

Then I looked out of the window and up at the sky.

'Thanks,' I said to the universe at large.

I thought back to the other near misses in my life and replayed images of them in my head. Hell, if I were a cat, I'd be dead by now!

My close calls started when I was five and living with my family in Belgium. As was the fad at the time, we had a large, heavy chandelier in the lounge. I was sitting under it in the middle of the room, watching the black and white version of Charles Dickens' *A Christmas Carol* on TV, so it was obviously that time of year.

The ghost of Christmas Future had just appeared, and it must have scared me as I jumped away from the television. Only a second later, the chandelier fell directly onto the spot where I had been sitting. My dad rushed over and scooped me up to get me out of the area.

The second time was with my older sister, Nicola, who has shared several strange experiences with me. She is older, fine-boned and has a much smaller frame than I. If we were toys, she'd be a china doll and I'd be an action man!

At the time, she still wore wide glasses that she hated. Her long reddish hair had turned brown and fell straight from its middle parting. Although she remained much more timid and pliable than I, she was starting to come out of her shell.

Nic and I had taken to playing on the flat roof of the shop attached to our house where both of our parents worked. We would role-play various characters, but especially enjoyed the game where one of us would play a fugitive and the other would be the cop hunting her down.

We took turns running and clambering up onto the ten-foot roof and then jumping off and rolling on the ground. Thinking back it was probably a bit dangerous, but at the time was just heaps of fun.

On this summer's day, we weren't on the roof but across the road at a house where two of our friends lived. We were playing in the front room on window seats when our friends' mother decided we should all go out for a walk. We happily did so as it was a glorious day and the idea of running across green open fields was appealing.

Later, as we returned, we were shocked to see an ambulance in front of our friends' house and police cars blocking the street. When we got closer we noticed that the window seats where we'd earlier been playing were now completely destroyed.

A car that had contained two young men had ploughed straight into it! If we hadn't gone for a walk, all four of us kids probably would not have survived.

My other close brushes with death occurred at ad hoc times as I got older. The last was in the mountains of Nepal where I'd journeyed for the second time after Adam died. He'd inspired me to visit originally and, on my return, I'd revelled in telling him all about my trip to Everest Base camp.

I made the second trip, an attempt to climb a mountain called Mera Peak, in memory of him. Although not technically difficult, it was in a region where the weather was especially brutal.

I was being sponsored for the trek to raise money for a charity run by the Himalayan Foundation, which put girls from rural Nepal through school.

Despite feeling good about raising money, I struggled a lot more physically and emotionally on the trek than the first one. After several weeks of walking to the region where Mera Peak sits magnificently in the clouds, we hiked to an area that was to become our base for a few days. From there we'd make the push to one final camp and aim for the summit starting in the dark, early hours of the morning in order to be at the top for sunrise.

The day before that final push, I started to get headaches and have trouble seeing. I felt sick and started to vomit. These were clear signs of altitude sickness. The guide sent me back from our practice hike with one of the sherpas, and I retreated to the warmth of my sleeping bag. I was asleep for a long time, and when I finally awoke the group had been back and had dinner. Not usually a tactile man, the guide came up and gave me a hug, clearly relieved that I'd made a recovery.

'I was worried you weren't going to make it,' he said. 'Or we'd have to take you down and fly you to hospital tomorrow.'

The other members of the group and especially my tent buddy who apparently had popped into the tent earlier and tried to rouse me, also seemed equally relieved to see me alive and well. Apparently I'd been sicker than I realised and had made a lucky recovery without having to descend in order to get thicker air (which is basically air with more oxygen in it).

The guide gave me the option to push for the summit the next day but then spent almost an hour counselling me against it. His fear was that I'd take sick again and a much-needed Sherpa would have to bring me back. If this happened there would be fewer sherpas to help the others, and it got much harder the higher up you went.

After losing Adam, I no longer had a fear of dying and, in fact, a part of me was disappointed at not having joined him that day. But as I sat dejected in my tent weighing the pros and cons, I realised that although I didn't mind if I never made it back, if someone else in the group got hurt because of me, I'd never forgive myself.

For that reason, the next morning when everyone got up before dawn for the two-day push to the summit, I joined them to wave them off. As it transpired, out of a group of ten only three made the summit and, the guide was pleased anyone made it at all.

Thinking of that incident and how I'd felt almost cheated of death up there, I realised, again, that I'd been wanting to die for a long time. But now, after my latest near miss, something had changed. I was relieved and exhilarated at being alive and dodging the falling sheds rather than cursing my survival instincts.

I found myself talking to Adam in the car.

'Shit, Adam. I could have been talking to you in person much sooner than I thought.

'I can't wait to see you again but I don't think I'm quite ready to join you now. I hope you don't mind, I really want to see Sam again.

'I'm guessing you're OK with that and, if it was you watching out for me back there, thank you.'

I felt his calming presence and breathed it in. I'd felt him a few times since his death. Once when I was really low, I was lying in bed weeping and asking him for a sign that he was still with me. It was after midnight and I'd been in bed for a while. As I was giving up and feeling even more dejected, the iPod downstairs started playing on its own. I wasn't scared. I knew it was the sign I'd asked for, and I thanked him for it.

I thought of Sam and knew that whether we were meant to have a relationship or not, it would never change the connection I had with Adam. Even in death, we were still soul mates.

I drove on thinking about Adam for a long time before glancing at the clock. Less than forty-eight hours after leaving Georgia, I was now only a short distance from San Diego. I was about to pull over and ring Sam when he called and asked where I was. I decided it was time to tell him the truth—I was going to need his address anyway!

He sounded so shocked that I had made it so far in such a short time and scolded me for not sleeping and resting properly. But then I could hear the excitement in his voice as he told me his address and worked out that I would be there within the hour.

I was so relieved and happy that he was also looking forward to seeing me again and sang along with the radio until I pulled up at his block of apartments.

Date #14: Sam – The Official Date in Las Vegas

As I got out of the car, suddenly all of my joy and confidence dissipated. I became really nervous as my inner doubting Thomas filled my mind with questions such as:

> *What if he doesn't like me after he spends more time with me?*
> *What if I don't like him again?*
> *What if the spark I felt on the first date and over the phone isn't there when I see him?*

Luckily, reality proved my doubts wrong. Sam was just as lovely as I remembered him, even more so. And he was just as excited to be spending more time with me as I was with him. He even insisted I stay with him until my conferences.

We hugged and chattered like excited children, and then he ran around full of nervous tension as he settled me in and told me where everything was so I could get some food and freshen up. Then he left for work. I showered and fell into his bed, feeling happier than I had literally in years.

The next few days, I wished away the daylight hours until he came home from work around 11 p.m. Once home, we'd have a late-night supper and gossip away merrily together.

Afterwards in bed, we traded secrets, insecurities, hopes and desires before coiling into one another. Sam seemed to know instinctively what to do or say to make me happy and feel secure.

From the start we completely clicked on an emotional and physical level and I realised this was partly because I trusted him more in that short time I'd known him than anyone I'd dated over the years since going out with Adam.

And, because of that, it was no surprise I fell in love with him faster and harder than I had ever before.

We enjoyed being with each other so much that we would spend most of our time, from him coming home from work to leaving again the next afternoon, in bed together.

When it came time for me to go to my conference, we didn't want to part company so soon, so he came to Las Vegas with me and became my official date for Nevada.

We spent hours walking along the strip, spotting Denny's signs, visiting the Coca-Cola shop and guessing at the backgrounds of the myriad of people ambling along the streets or frittering away their money in the casinos.

I will never like the vibe or baseness that is so evident in Vegas, but I hardly noticed it whilst with Sam. I felt blissfully happy. Sam seemed to feel the same and we arranged for me to go back to his apartment at the end of the coaching conference and the Loral Langemeier event.

When I returned to San Diego Sam and I spent as much time together as we could. We discussed my travel plans and he helped me reorganise the route. Originally I was going to head north up the west coast but given we were heading into October Sam suggested I cover the colder east coast first before it really got cold. He knew the country much better than I, so I heeded his advice and booked myself on a flight to Baltimore that left a week later.

I met his family and they were all so welcoming that it was hard not to relax and enjoy being with them. I could see why Sam was so well-balanced and had all of his priorities straight.

Time seemed to fly by and my departure date loomed large. Sam and I had agreed that I should continue with my dates and follow through with my plans. Despite integrity being a big part of my Positive Change Formula, I was having serious doubts about continuing with the dates.

Shortly before I left, Sam and I drove up to my friend Lorence's in Los Angeles to drop off my big suitcase, which he was babysitting for me given I was now going to be taking a lot more domestic flights and needed to travel light in order to avoid paying the hefty baggage fees. On the drive back, I couldn't help but blurt out my feelings.

'I don't want to go,' I said quickly as I looked across at him.

'You have to go,' he replied. 'You have to finish the dates and write your book.' He smiled at me. 'After selling the copies, you've got to see it through,' he said, throwing back what I'd told him in the past.

'What if I meet someone else?' I was hoping to goad him.

'If you meet someone you want to kiss, that's fine, and if you want to go out with them, again, that's okay, too.'

That was not the answer I was looking for and I rapidly grew worried and unsure about what was happening between us.

I'd thought we were now in a relationship and he just wanted me to finish the dates because he knew how serious I was about the commitment I'd made. But suddenly he was saying that he was fine not only with my dating other people, but also with my having a relationship with them. Something had shifted.

I was scared to check my read of this new situation but given my personality, I couldn't help but put the question to him. He danced around the subject a little, but after a time he came clean and told me what I didn't want to hear, but what I was beginning to see clearly was the case.

Although I felt an intense connection with Sam and would have happily moved my entire world to be with him, he didn't feel the same way. He admitted that he'd worked it out a day or two before and was going to tell me after I'd left.

He gave me the usual, 'I'm not ready for a relationship' crap, which just made me angry. It wasn't that he wasn't ready for a relationship he just didn't want one with me. I'd used the line before so I knew the truth of the statement!

My inner critic went into overdrive. I cursed myself for being such an idiot and letting my defences down so quickly. I told myself that, of course he didn't want to be with me, why would anyone want such a screwed-up mess? I told myself I didn't deserve to be happy or loved and that this was inevitable. All of my doubts and insecurities found a voice.

I wanted to stay somewhere else that final night, but Sam pleaded with me not to. He seemed genuinely upset that he'd hurt me so much.

However, that night I couldn't feel anything but my own anger and hurt, and I couldn't hear anything but my inner voice telling me, 'I told you so'. All I wanted to do was run away and hide.

It seemed like the longest night of my life, and I was so eager to leave that I rose early in the morning. I'd packed my bag hastily when we'd arrived back at the apartment so reorganised things as Sam made breakfast and tried to engage me in polite conversation.

I would happily have headed straight to the airport, hours earlier than my departure time, but I could sense that Sam was desperately trying to make peace with me before I left and he wanted to drive me to the airport himself.

I was still in love with him and couldn't bear to see him looking so miserable and uncomfortable, so I tried to appease his sense of guilt, even though it was the last thing I wanted to do.

My bad luck raised its ugly head when, to add insult to injury, on the way to the airport, Sam accidentally took the wrong exit and caused me to miss my plane.

When he finally dropped me off at the airport, I stood at the check-in counter and cried.

A Military Operation

As I stood at the counter crying, I also wanted to scream, throw things and curl up in a ball. However, being acutely conscious of today's security, I followed the safer route and, after the kind and patient counter ladies gave me other flight options, I went to get myself a drink and think things over.

I sipped at my orange juice then took a few deep cleansing breaths as I closed my eyes.

Okay, so I was hurt, angry and bewildered, but I no longer had any temptations and my integrity would not be tested further by Sam. I still had my plan and at least this way I was free to meet the man who did want to spend the rest of his life with me.

Maybe this was a good thing? It sure didn't feel like it now, but I had learnt through experience that everything, including life, is temporary.

Maybe if Sam hadn't done what he did, I would not have finished my journey and not only missed out on a host of new experiences, but ended up ashamed for not remaining true to myself and my promise.

Whatever the reason, the universe had decided that Sam was not the one for me. I had to believe it was because there was someone better around the corner.

The ladies at the airline counter had offered me a seat on a flight to Baltimore that left at 11 p.m., ten hours after the flight I was originally booked on. So, I went back and took them up on it.

I took a bus into the city, found a coffee shop, bought a large mocha and some food, and settled in to use their free wifi and organise the next few weeks of my life.

I already had several dates organised so the first part of my itinerary remained the same, but the rest changed completely.

When I had been reworking the trip with Sam, I had organised a leisurely tour down, and then back up, the east coast all the way through New England. However, in an act of defiance to Sam, and because I now just wanted to get the dates over with, I reviewed ways I could cram in as many of them as logistically possible before I was due to leave for my short break in Mexico.

Thanks to Google maps, I worked out driving times between states and figured out a haphazard route. I looked at every possible flight variation imaginable jotting down days, times and costs in my notepad. Writing down every day between now and my flight out of the country I realised there was no way I would make all fifty states and resigned myself to the fact I would have to come back at some point in 2012 to finish them off.

However, after a brief phone call to the travel company I had booked my kayaking trip with, I had cancelled the kayaking and changed my Mexican flight to a later date. This provided me with extra days in the US and time for three extra dates.

Although I was going to make several flights and jump around the country a lot my new itinerary worked. It was not the neatest or the most scenic of ways I could cross the country, and it certainly wasn't the cheapest, but sticking to my financial budget was not my highest goal.

In fact, my upcoming trip was going to be a whirlwind through twenty-seven states and Washington D.C. It would be like a military operation. There was no room for error or lateness. I smiled. I always like a challenge and this was certainly one.

While concentrating on making plans I'd kept my feelings at bay, but when I got on the plane that would take me away from Sam, I suddenly took a deep intake of breath. Although making the plans had helped me feel more in control I still wanted to cry. Instead of burying my hurt this time, in the darkness of the plane, I turned to face the window and wept.

Although I didn't want to date anyone else when I had a broken heart, I told myself I needed to focus on two positives. The first was that I now knew that I could fall in love again. The second was that I had a recent benchmark to which I could compare other men.

I didn't intend to compare and contrast their personalities or looks with Sam's, but I did want to hold the memory of how he made me feel and how connected we were so that I could gauge whether I felt that with anyone else and if it would be worth making plans to return to see them the following year. I had decided that even if I fell head over heels for the next guy I met, I was NOT going to divert from my plan again and waste time unnecessarily.

My itinerary had me travelling from Maryland to D.C. through Virginia, on to North and South Carolina, and then flying up to New York. I'd get a car and drive to Pennsylvania, New Jersey, and Delaware before retracing my steps back to New York City.

From there I'd fly to Wisconsin and do a loop to Illinois, Indiana, Michigan and back. Another flight out of Wisconsin would take me to Minnesota and just across the border to North Dakota. Then I would travel across to Idaho and down to Utah.

From Utah I'd take another flight to Nebraska and then complete another loop that took me from Omaha through Iowa on to South Dakota, where I would briefly cross the border to Montana and Wyoming, before driving back to Omaha.

Out of Omaha I was flying down to West Virginia, getting a car, and crossing the country again through Ohio, Kentucky, Missouri, Kansas and ending up in Colorado.

From there, I'd go to Hawaii for two days and then take a week's rest in Mexico. Having cancelled the kayaking I'd planned the travel company had now booked me into a resort for a week of pampering.

When I finally got off the plane in Baltimore late that night, I tried to shrug off any thoughts of Sam and concentrated on my plan. It had been a productive day. I fell asleep at the hotel later, sure in the knowledge that there were lots more adventures ahead.

Maryland

Up until this point, I'd met many of my dates in shorts and a t-shirt because the weather had been so wonderful, but as summer had turned to fall and it was getting cool even in San Diego, Sam had warned me to pack some of my warmer gear as I was going to need it. I had pulled out the couple of jeans, shirts and long sleeved tops which were in my case and stuffed them into my smaller backpack. They would have to do. I would be clean and casual but still my attire could not be classed as suitable for work or fancy restaurants.

This suited me perfectly as, to be honest, I've never been comfortable dressing up. Despite a couple of corrective operations on my feet when I was a teenager, I still found even normal shoes painful, so heels were a definite no-no.

To ensure my dates were not surprised by my appearance, every time I planned a meeting, I used the excuse that I was travelling and had little going-out gear to make sure we met in a suitably casual place.

I had been counselled by many of my girlfriends that this attire would surely kill any interest a man had in me, but to the contrary, none of my dates had cared about my lack of a dress or make-up and accessories. In fact, up until that point, all of them had asked me for a second date.

Date #15: Andrew – Jumping Straight Back On The Horse

My first date back was with a chef named Andrew. He was a little chubby and, with hair that was beginning to grey, he looked every bit the ten years older than me that he was. He was very quietly spoken and laid back, but somehow I felt uncomfortable and a little aloof.

We had a perfectly pleasant evening but I was feeling a bit disconnected. I tried to engage so I matched and mirrored his tone, energy and body language, but I felt less and less interested.

At the end of the date I was surprised that he asked me out again. It appeared he'd had a different experience than I had, and even the small amount of effort I'd made was enough.

This intrigued me so when I got back to the hotel, I took the time to think about what I was doing to get such a great hit rate and I drafted a quick list.

The first thing I did was to set expectations before we met and be very clear upfront not to expect me in a dress and make-up. That in itself meant I was dressed in attire I felt comfortable in, which probably reflected in my behaviour somehow.

Second, because I had so many dates lined up, I also went into each date knowing that if this man wasn't Mr. Right that was okay because I was meeting someone else very soon anyway. Consequently I was more relaxed than I would have been if I were desperate to make a connection or just had the one date.

Third, until Sam dumped me I was happy and confident, and this really seemed to draw people in.

Fourth, I allowed the other person to talk a fair amount more than I did and was genuinely interested in them, which likely meant they felt listened to and important—nice for all of us!

And finally, I matched their energy and tone and mirrored some of the words they used, which seemed to put them at ease and build rapport quickly. At the end of several dates, many guys remarked that they felt they'd known me for years or had something in common with me despite my not necessarily saying very much or divulging much of my own personal information.

I had originally learned about some of these techniques when I was reading books on body language in an effort to improve my negotiation and networking skills. I guess now I was doing them unwittingly as I sat back surprised at all of the actions I was taking to unconsciously steer my date in a direction I wanted him to go.

Was I being manipulative in using these techniques on a date? I felt a little guilty about it and wondered how my dates would have gone without this unconscious assistance. I also knew that long term I probably wouldn't use these techniques with them on a daily basis. I certainly didn't use them with my friends. That raised the question, was I giving them the wrong impression of who I am? Would they like me anyway?

Washington D.C.

Despite now knowing what helped my previous dates go well, the next few went poorly, and so much of it was my fault. Conscious of what I had been doing, I was now very aware of my behaviour and so became uncomfortable and uptight in an effort not to manipulate my date into liking me. As I was spending a lot of time travelling and less resting so my stress levels were rising. Plus I was still feeling protective of myself and guarded as a result of Sam's rejection.

Because I was stressed, upset, self-conscious or in a hurry, I made less of an effort and this was certainly showing as none of the men I met in Washington D.C., Virginia, North or South Carolina asked me out again.

Date #16: Luke – A Walk In The Park

In Washington D.C., I'd had dinner with Luke, who was younger than I am and we'd then taken an evening stroll around some of the memorials. Given he was working in politics in a similar job to mine previously, we had a lot in common, but instead of this bringing us together it had the opposite effect.

Luke got intensely competitive about where he was on the ladder compared to where I had been. If I'd been in the mood, I might have allowed him to feel superior, but I really wasn't, and why should I, anyway? I slapped him down verbally several times, leaving the poor guy reeling and obviously feeling insecure.

Probably feeling a need to prove himself he started to tell me some confidential details about what was going on in local politics. Many people would have lapped this up, but I stopped him short. After years of working in public service, I had never confided confidential information to anyone outside of work. It was part of the job and I reminded him of this.

We walked the remainder of the circuit in silence. It reminded me of Canberra where I'd worked and I enjoyed the memories it was evoking. I suspect he was reflecting on other things and, needless to say, I think he was quite relieved the date was over when we got back to where we'd started. He fled into the night.

Virginia, North Carolina, South Carolina, New York, Pennsylvania, New Jersey and Delaware

Dates #17 – 23: Too Many To Mention

In the last quarter of the year in the Northern hemisphere, it was beginning to turn cold, and the grey, rainy days were getting to me.

The few warm clothes I had in my backpack were not warm enough and I'd chosen to leave my heavy hiking boots and warm socks behind in my suitcase at Lorence's in an effort to minimise the weight. I was berating myself about this but feeling loathe to buy anything more to drag around with me, although I did invest in some lightweight closed-toe shoes to keep my feet from turning into blocks of ice.

My discomfort was probably another reason the dates I went on didn't go well.

It didn't help that one of the guys was married and hadn't even bothered to take his wedding ring off. Until I noticed it, we had been having a nice evening enjoying a good meal at a restaurant on Virginia Beach, overlooking the sea. Of course, when I spotted the ring on his finger I had to ask.

To his credit he didn't deny it. He admitted he had left his wife and kids about an hour's drive away to come on the date with me. He said he just wanted to have a good night out and some fun.

Reminded of Kyle and how he had treated me—not to mention the woman he was still married to—I snapped. My blood boiled as I told him that I was sure his wife probably wanted a good night out and some fun too. But obviously she wasn't a lying cheat like he was.

Open-mouthed he sat in the middle of the restaurant clearly unsure what to do as I jerked upright, grabbed my jacket and stormed out, giving him no opportunity to reply to my verbal attack.

Another guy, Todd, who I met in Philadelphia put me in *my* place when, after several attempts at making conversation and simply getting grunts or one-word answers, I tried one final time to improve the situation.

'This isn't going very well, is it? You seem distracted,' I said.

He replied with the longest sentence he uttered the whole twenty minutes we were together.

'Nope,' he said. 'I just don't find you very interesting, or really very attractive either.'

It was my turn to sit open-mouthed. Unsure whether it was normal etiquette to be so direct in the US or not, my British sensibilities were aghast at his rudeness. I was speechless for a few seconds then retorted, 'Let's not waste any more of each other's time then.'

I got up, gathered my things and left, heading on a little walk around the so-called City of Brotherly love. I reflected on the conversation I'd just had with Todd. If he'd had any sense of my feelings, I might have considered his honesty refreshing, no matter how rudely delivered. However, just as I was building up my self-image again, he had torn at it and left me feeling wounded and vulnerable.

As I was wandering aimlessly about I found myself outside the former state penitentiary which was already having nightly Halloween events despite it only being early October. As I walked past people in garish make-up, I stopped and turned around.

I'm not sure whether this reaction was because I'm originally British and we feel the need to queue everywhere or not but I dutifully stood at the end of the line of people who had also decided they wanted to go to 'Fright Night'.

A young couple joined the queue behind me and after a while, seeing that I was not with any of the people standing ahead of us, struck up a conversation. After politely probing whether or not I was indeed there by myself and ascertaining that was the case, the man asked whether I had any idea what Fright Night at the state pen was all about.

I admitted I had absolutely no clue what to expect except that, it would probably include people trying to frighten me. He had obviously been before and explained that once in the prison, we would be guided along through one prison block to another with no escape and no choice other than to follow the path to the end.

'Would you like to stick with us on the way around?' his girlfriend volunteered kindly.

'That would be great thanks.'

'Are you a screamer?' the boyfriend asked his voice full of excitement.

I blinked at him confused at what I momentarily perceived to be yet another inappropriate conversation that evening. And then, I realised he was asking if I was likely to scream on the way around Fright Night, not during sex!

Relieved, I replied 'I have absolutely no idea. Let's find out!'

My reaction when a costumed man jumped out and grabbed me from the darkness probably disappointed him since, instead of letting out a blood curdling scream, I reverted back to being terribly, terribly British.

'O my, what fabulous make-up you have on!' I gushed, and then giggled.

The costumed man went on to find his next victim, and I shuffled on through the darkened corridors decked out with secret rooms and more people lurking in the recesses, but still no scream had passed my lips when we finally walked back out of the penitentiary onto the streets about an hour later.

As I got in the car and drove back to the hotel, I reflected that the evening hadn't turned out so badly after all and Fright Night had actually been *frightfully* good. In fact, the scariest thing that happened to me that evening was that, although I knew Todd earlier was in the wrong for his behaviour, I had allowed it to negatively affect my ego and confidence levels.

By the time I left New York on the plane to Wisconsin, I was feeling sad and dejected.

Wisconsin, Indiana, Michigan

After several disastrous dates, I made a great effort to shift my mood.

When I got to Milwaukee, I took some time out for me. I enjoyed girl time with the ladies in the hairdressers who I chatted to about my trip. As with many other people who I had spoken to at conferences, on planes or other venues about the reason for my US tour, they all exclaimed how brave I was to be not just travelling the US on my own but dating so many men along the way.

They thought it was brave, risky and romantic, and each shared with me some of their experiences and their own pearls of wisdom about dating.

'What do all your dates think about being one of the fifty?' the lady giving me my massage had asked.

With my face squeezed into the hole in the massage table as I was staring at the floor, I answered 'Actually, unless they specifically ask I haven't told them.'

As she applied more pressure to my calf muscles she said, 'Isn't that a little dishonest?'

'Maybe,' I replied in a muffled voice 'Although I do mention on my profile that I'm travelling through each of the US states looking for love. I just decided at the start that I didn't want the men to feel competitive or self-conscious about the date. And I didn't want to be talking about me or my travels and dominating the conversations each time. I could be doing the wrong thing but I thought this way was the best route to take.'

She moved to work out some of the tension I'd been holding in my neck and shoulders as she gave me her opinion on the matter.

I listened and considered her point of view. I suppose some people may question my integrity and honesty towards the men I was dating, and that was a fair enough point of view. However, they didn't have to date them.

As I am genuinely looking for a partner, I don't want men to date me purely to appear in a book. I want them to have a real interest in me and be themselves when I meet them—otherwise how can I make any real assessment as to personality and compatibility? No, I understood where she was coming from but I would choose to maintain my course of action. The last thing I needed was to attract any more nutters, I was trying to limit the potential through my ten standard questions, not encourage them by broadcasting the fact that I'm dating fifty men in fifty states upfront!

As I was laying on the massage table I considered the nine dates I'd now had since leaving Sam. They had gone by in a blur and I realised that I'd slipped into my old habit of throwing myself into work... at least

I wasn't throwing myself at it seeing as I was now obviously regarding each of my dates as work!

Reflecting on this, I knew that in order to enjoy this journey, I needed to reframe my thinking. This wasn't work. This was fun. My goals for this trip were not to work even though I'd now agreed to write about my adventures. My goals for this particular part of my journey were to reconnect with others and try to find my Mr. Right.

Holding that clarity in my mind as I got off the massage table, I went on my next few dates and, surprise! I began to enjoy them again—at least three out of the four anyway.

The men in Indiana and Illinois particularly stood out, one for a good reason, the other, well, ahem...

Date #26: Jacob – Moonwalking in Gary, Indiana

One of the nice dates was Jacob, an African-American, six-foot two, skinny guy whose clothes were falling off him, but who wore his wide smile perfectly. Our date was in Gary, Indiana, and any music buffs would know exactly why I did this.

I did feel a little guilty that I specifically went on a date in Gary so I could get Jacob to take me to see Michael Jackson's house and schools, but, hey, I like him... MJ that is, I didn't have an opinion on Jacob just yet!

I don't mean to be rude to the locals of Gary—everyone I met was welcoming—but, blimey, the town itself is a hole! The houses were all small, old and in dire need of repair, there were pot holes in the roads too big to manoeuvre around and the schools I saw looked like they hadn't been renovated in decades. I can see why MJ's father pushed them so much to get out of there.

The locals were obviously still proud of their famous son. In the front garden of the house where MJ was born stood a large, black granite stone in which was etched a depiction of him striking one of the dance poses he was known for.

It's good that Jacob knew where the house was as there is no way I would have found it otherwise. Unlike Graceland with all of its show there were no sign posts to point the way or shops selling MJ paraphernalia anywhere near the house. The whole neighbourhood looked rundown and deserted. It was pretty sad.

Jacob was lots of fun and outside the house he bust out some MJ moves doing a pretty good moon walk and rather energetically grabbing his crotch and whooping! He made me laugh.

He came across as a bit of a hustler, although I don't think he would hurt a fly. He was 'between' jobs and when he found out I had chosen to give mine up he kept going on about how crazy I was.

'Waddya mean?' he had screeched, when I casually told him I had decided to resign and take a year off. 'You weren't fired? You chose to stop work?'

'Yeah,' I shrugged. 'I needed a break.'

'A break is a two week vacation, lady... not a year!' came his reply as he jiggled his head and gesticulated in disbelief.

I gave him an apologetic smile, now more than a little embarrassed for being in such a privileged position to have chosen to leave my job. I shrugged again, 'Ahhh well. It's done now I can't turn back the clock. May as well enjoy the time I have, right? Life isn't a dress rehearsal.'

'Lady, you're nuts,' he said seriously and then broke into a grin. 'I like it!'

I was glad this date in Gary was just a pit-stop on the way to Chicago since I wouldn't like to have stayed long. Despite Jacob being full of beans and heaps of fun, the atmosphere in the town was pretty depressing.

I expected to encounter poverty in the third world countries I visited but seeing it in the US somehow seemed to make it harsher as I compared this area with Pasadena in California, for example. It was the same country but the stark contrast between the housing and standard of living was shocking.

Jacob was a good guy and I felt badly for him that he and so many of his friends were faced with such a difficult existence and uncertain future. And yet here he was smiling and having fun, I had to respect him for his spirit and resilience!

Illinois

Date #27: Roger – The Job Interview

Ever since the first film I saw that was set in Chicago, I have wanted to visit. The views of the Harbour and the panoramic shots of the city made it look so tempting. Although now I think about it, it did look grey much of the time, as it was the day of my date.

I arrived in the afternoon, and the weather got worse as the day went on. By the time of my date, it was blowing a gale and the rain had set in. Because the cost of parking was astronomical, Roger, my date, had told me to park in the city and walk to meet him at the famous North Pier. However, since I wasn't dressed for this kind of weather nor did I have any clothes that would protect me from the gale I chose to spend the money.

I met Roger outside a popcorn shop. I couldn't believe a shop could only sell different types of popcorn. How cool is that! I made a mental note to return after dinner for a packet of the caramel.

When I met Roger, I noticed that he was dressed even more scruffily than I was without having the excuse of travelling the US with only a handful of clothes in a backpack.

Looking at him, you could have been forgiven for thinking he was homeless, but as I knew from his profile and as he told me in great detail later, he had his own place and was one of the lucky ones in the US to be employed.

Had he been in Jacob's shoes, I could have forgiven him his lank blonde hair with dandruff on the shoulders of his faded black leather jacket. However, the reality was he had simply not made an effort.

The only thing bright and shiny about Roger was his light blue eyes, which stood out on his thin, scrawny face. The rest of him looked dull and unwashed and he even smelled like he hadn't showered in a while even though he had a recent soak in the rain on his walk down.

He met me with, 'Wow, you are prettier in person. I'm intimidated now,' a comment whose tone left me wondering if he was being serious or not.

Given his body odour, I suggested a walk on the pier, but unfortunately we had to head back in pretty quickly as the weather was so atrocious it was difficult to stand upright and walk at the same time. There was no chance of hearing Roger even when he shouted, which I had, even after this short time, decided was a good thing.

As with the majority of my dates, I asked him if he wouldn't mind taking a couple of photos of me given I was in Chicago and wanted a visual reminder of the day. Trying to pretend it was warm so my family and friends on Facebook would be jealous, I failed miserably in pulling it off as I hunched against the cold and smiled thinly whilst he took the shots.

We bid a hasty retreat back to the shelter of the pier and decided McDonalds was as good a place as any to have dinner.

Roger and I both ordered a Big Mac meal, both of which I paid for as Roger pushed his hands further into his pockets and looked nonchalantly away when the girl behind the counter announced the cost.

As we sat down he started jabbering on at me whilst he unwrapped his burger and fries. He continued talking at me, rather than to me, as we ate. He neither gave me time to make a comment nor, it seemed, needed one as his continued chattering. His attitude reminded me of the English guy, Nathan from New Mexico and I wondered whether he was going to bombard me with texts and calls after the date had ended too.

However, Roger was scary in a whole other way. It turned out he was big into computers and he let me know that by asking me after we had settled in, if I was indeed *the Melanie Brocklehurst, Head of...* he was addressing. If he had wanted to freak me out by this comment, it had the desired effect as I hadn't shared my last name nor told anyone where I worked before we met. My stomach lurched, 'O God what have I got myself into and how can I get out of it quickly', I thought pensively, and instinctively looked around at all the ways out of the restaurant.

Unaware of my reaction, Roger continued on proudly explaining how he used to be a computer hacker and had been hired for those skills in his job working for some computer security firm. He described to me how he had taken an image of my face from the photos on the dating site and somehow found other matching photos of me elsewhere on the net to work out exactly who I was. I think I was supposed to be impressed but instead I was just highly perturbed.

He then spent what felt like hours, but was probably only forty minutes, talking in computer jargon and acronyms about the personal projects he was working on. I nodded politely but understood little.

Halfway through his monologue I wondered where all this was going. Given his speech was quick and he seemed slightly nervous it felt like he was auditioning for something, but I wasn't sure what. At the end, he stopped and looked at me expectantly.

When I continued to sit there dumbstruck he asked, 'So, do you think any of my projects have merit?'

I hedged my bets. 'Ummm, maybe', I said.

'So you'll take the specs and information to your company for me then and see if the bigwigs are interested?' His tone was a little too demanding for my liking.

Hell no! Even if I were still working for the company, I wouldn't do that. Dates are NOT to be mixed up with job interviews. Trying to keep the annoyance out of my voice, I told him that I couldn't help him as I no longer worked for the company.

'Well, why didn't you tell me that earlier?' he retorted, clearly frustrated.

'If you read my profile then you would have spotted that I am having a year off,' I countered, unapologetically.

'So I just walked here and wasted my time when you can't help me?' he said with an accusing look.

'Errrm. Seeing as this was meant to be a date and not a job interview, I have no idea why you are angry at me.' I replied incredulously.

At the start of the date I was going to offer him a lift back into the city to save him the walk but decided against it now, grateful that I hadn't been given the opportunity throughout our meeting to open my mouth and make the suggestion.

If he wanted to be rude and thoughtless, fine, I could too. I stood up as a sign that the discussion was over. 'I have to use the bathroom. Have a safe walk home' was my parting remark as I picked up my bag and walked away.

I had planned to get a bed in Chicago for the night but changed my mind. I walked back to the popcorn shop and bought myself the largest size caramel popcorn I could, and headed to the car. I drove back to Milwaukee, flipping a bird at the city of Chicago when it was in my rear-view mirror.

By the time I got back to Milwaukee and settled into a hotel, I realised I had probably been a little rash leaving Chicago without giving it a real chance. My overreaction was probably because I was still a little tired with all of the travelling. On a positive note as I'd now driven back to where I was flying out from, I could have a lie in and take it easy before my early afternoon flight the next day.

The next morning as I was lounging in bed, I reflected on my past four dates. Okay, so they hadn't been the best but that didn't matter. With three out of four, I'd managed to engage with the guys again and have a little fun.

And even thinking about Roger, I couldn't help but feel a little sorry for the guy, who obviously had no social skills whatsoever. That being said, his rudeness and mishandling of the situation still rankled, so I didn't feel too badly. I know us Brits are probably a little too prim and proper but I cannot abide rudeness, the abhorrence of which was probably bred into my lineage centuries ago!

Spotting my unconscious reactions I again turned to review my new conscious behaviours. By purposely deciding to be open and enjoy myself again this had really changed how I was viewing the dates and myself. And, indeed, may again have changed the outcome of the dates themselves. Because, the majority of the time I'd had lots of fun and so had the guys I met, I was again being asked for second dates.

I pondered this. It was a useful thing to know. I made a mental note to try and use this technique of changing my perception to change circumstances at other times when I may need to, like during an interview or in another stressful situation. Who knows, it could even help me in fulfilling some of the other goals on the list I had drafted.

Again, I pulled the list out and reminded myself of the purpose of this trip and my year off. 'You can do it, Mel' I muttered quietly and with conviction. 'You have set your course – now don't waver from it. That is what tenacity and integrity are all about.'

Minnesota, North Dakota, Idaho, Utah

When I got to Minneapolis, Minnesota, I had some time to myself before my date at the famous Mall of America that night with Roberto.

Having decided in Wisconsin to have a massage and find somewhere to tint my eyebrows as my eyes had really disappeared now that my brows were a light red colour again, I had done a quick search on a couple of websites and made some calls from the hotel.

Confirming what time my flight got in and how far the massage places were from the airport I found one that had an appointment at a time that suited me.

When I got there, the massage I had was brilliant and the masseuse really worked out the kinks in my neck and jaw, both of which needed some work.

Time on her table reminded me of Daisy, who had started off as my masseuse and later become a great friend and surrogate mum to me, and, now to my dog, Jessie. Her massages as well as her generosity of spirit have earned her my lasting friendship and business as well as that of scores of other loyal clients and friends.

I realised I was a little homesick for Australia. Overall, I was enjoying the US and the dates but despite us allegedly sharing a common language many of the words used to describe everyday things was different and jarring to my ear.

The amount of nouns I had heard used as a verb was astounding. It was like Americans just made words up on the spot! *Incentivise* instead of to create incentive, *trialling* a new product, it *impacted* me to hear such things! My dad was a stickler for grammar and the correct use of a word and his attitude, I found, had rubbed off.

'Stop it, Mel', I counselled myself. 'You are just making yourself angry thinking about it.' And then I thought, 'Why not put what you have just learnt about changing your perception to good use and have some fun? Introduce them to your favourite words!'

From that point on, I decided the Yanks really needed to embrace the words *Bollocks* and *Fuckwit* and to hell with it I would create a new verb too, *Fuckwittage*! 'I've never heard of such *fuckwittery* in all of my life', I muttered to myself and chortled gleefully. I was going to enjoy this!

Thinking about one of the old work meetings I used to attend, I imagined the American senior execs getting annoyed and blurting out, 'Don't talk such bollocks, you fuckwit!' O the power of language!

Two of the most apt, descriptive and pleasurable words that I say with gusto when I am annoyed introduced into the American vernacular, now that would be fun! Ahhh, I felt better already.

I asked Jess, the masseuse, where I could get my eyelashes tinted and feeling happier with my new found purpose, I set off.

In Australia, all of the malls have beauticians who will provide you with an eyebrow wax and tint in as little as thirty minutes, so I thought finding somewhere to have this done would be easy. However, Jess hadn't mentioned that I actually needed to go to a hairdresser *not* a nail salon. What should have been simple became difficult.

After running around the mall, I finally found a girl willing to give it a shot. I went in the back of the nail salon and lay on the bed ready for my treatment. I asked for dark brown but warned her not to leave the colour on too long and with that I promptly fell asleep. It is not my usual practice to do this but a mixture of exhaustion after all of the travelling and relaxation after the massage proved to be a lethal combination.

This turned out to be a big mistake as I woke when my eyebrows were being rubbed rather more vigorously than should be necessary. My eyes shot open and I asked if everything was alright. The girl covered pretty well, but it was evident that she was a little panicked.

'Umm. They are pretty dark but they will lighten up in a few days,' she said.

I asked for a mirror and wished I hadn't when I saw my face. My eyebrows were jet black! Red hair, pink skin and jet black eyebrows—I looked like Coco the Clown without the need of make-up!

I took a deep breath and tried not to cry. Mindful that I'd overreacted the day before I didn't get angry. I gave the girl a tight smile, thanked her and left the shop, quickly putting on my sunglasses despite being inside a mall.

I got into the car and took another look in the mirror. It looked even worse in natural light. Shit! Of my many faults, vanity is not one of them, but the thought of meeting a date looking like this made me feel sick. Plus, according to his photos Roberto was pretty hot, and I was already having self-image issues after Sam's rejection.

So I rang Roberto from the car and tried to fast track out of the date. He asked why the change of heart and at least I was honest. I told him I had a cosmetic incident. Probably not the best way of describing it and it only served to pique his interest. I ended up telling him about my eyebrows and he thought it was just plain funny.

He asked if I was still leaving the next day, and I replied in the affirmative.

'Well that's it, then,' he told me, 'we have to meet up tonight. Don't worry you can keep your sunglasses on!'

Date #28: Roberto – The Restorer Of Faith

When I met him outside the Sea Life Aquarium in the Mall of America (they have an aquarium and a theme park in there!) my stomach lurched as he was gorgeous! He looked like the tennis player, Roger Federer, although Roberto is from Argentina not Switzerland.

Normally, I would have been over the moon but my heart sank. I couldn't believe I was turning up to a date with a super hot guy looking like a female version of Groucho Marx. I cursed under my breath but decided now was the time to fake it. I put on a happy smile and confidently shook Roberto's hand.

It sounds a bit odd meeting at a mall but it was the biggest tourist attraction in the state from what I'd read and it turned out to be quite pleasant meandering around.

After a very enjoyable stroll and brief history lesson about the area, Roberto suggested we try at least one ride in the theme park. I reluctantly agreed.

'You'll have to take your sunglasses off though,' Roberto remarked gleefully. 'Come on then,' he coaxed. 'Show me your eyebrows I have been dying to see them.'

I tried to laugh it off and get out of taking my sunnies off, but he was really sweet about it and since he knew what had happened there was no point trying to hide it.

Hesitantly, I took off my sunnies. He smiled and I couldn't help but grin coyly at him.

And then, he did something that I completely did not expect. He took my face, looked at me and gave me a long kiss. To say you could have knocked me down with a feather would be an understatement.

He told me that he was having a wonderful time and that if I came back through Minneapolis he really wanted to see me again, black eyebrows included! He gave me another kiss, put his arm round me, and we went on the first of many rides in the theme park.

After that I did not once think about my dodgy eyebrows or Sam. Roberto managed to make me forget all of these things and I found my self-image inflate with every moment I spent with him. Hmmm... he was dreamy, and he liked me for me, black eyebrows included! Ahhh, Roberto!

I'm afraid to say that none of the dates in the rest of this group of states were anything in comparison to Roberto. I was seriously tempted to go back and see him again, but I'd made sure that was impossible with the crazy travel schedule I'd organised.

Still, Roberto called me several times in the days after we met to check how I was going and see if my eyebrows were any lighter. I would have loved to see him again and told him so, but explained that I was due to visit another twelve states, Mexico and my family in the UK before Christmas.

I promised myself that I would not alter my schedule for anyone, so I had to trust that if he was the guy for me we'd keep in touch and see each other again.

Omaha, Iowa, South Dakota, Montana, Wyoming, West Virginia, Ohio, Kentucky, Missouri, Kansas and Colorado... Phew!

The rest of the eleven dates on the US mainland seemed to go by quickly, but I was now having fun again and enjoying seeing so much of America.

For this last pass through the US, since I had such a short time in each state, I tried to ensure that my dates took me somewhere special. I wanted to make the most of the time I had left.

So far I'd walked through D.C. and seen the memorials, visited Virginia Beach, New York City, the North Pier in Chicago, Michael Jackson's house in Indiana, and so on.

Dates #34-36: Toby – Banter And Bickering In The Badlands

In South Dakota, with my date Toby, I saw the Badlands, Mount Rushmore and the Crazy Horse Memorial.

Toby worked in the hospitality industry near Mount Rushmore and didn't usually get two days off in a row so I was lucky that on this occasion he did and was willing to spend both days with a lady from another country he had never met.

Toby wasn't my usual type. He had mousy hair, which could do with a good cut. He was gangly (lean from hiking and his other outdoor adventures) and he wore glasses because he 'just couldn't get on with contact lenses' despite many attempts. But his appearance didn't matter a jot when I got to know him. Toby was adorable!

I picked Toby up outside a Starbucks he referred me to and he directed me from there. We first went to Mount Rushmore and stopped on the way up for the mandatory photo. Toby was aghast when I stepped out of the car and took my hoodie off.

'What are you doing? It's really cold today!'

'Don't worry I'll put my hoodie back on between shots I promise,' I laughingly replied. 'I just need it to look hot and sunny for the folks back home. Can't have them thinking I'm freezing my ass off!'

'Why? You are!' he retorted.

'I know that, but they don't! It's always cold, miserable and rainy in the UK I need to give them something happy to look at!'

He dutifully took the photos and I dutifully put my hoodie back on when we got back in the car.

We then drove up to the site of Mount Rushmore itself, which is controlled to ensure that there is no way to park without paying.

I paid for the parking and both our entrance fees, which Toby got very upset about as he tried to force money into my hand when we were walking from the car to the main entrance.

'Please take it,' he pleaded. 'A lady shouldn't pay on a date. It's just not right.'

'Seriously, Toby, you are doing me the favour by visiting sites that I'm sure you've been to hundreds of times on your day off.'

After I flatly refused to take his money, he told me that he was not going to any more sites unless he could pay in a sulky half-joking manner.

'OK', I said. 'You can pay for Crazy Horse but neither of us need pay at Badlands because I have an annual National Parks pass that I picked up with my mate Rachael earlier on in my trip.'

'Done,' he said, 'but we're using *my* annual pass for Badlands!'

We continued our friendly banter and bickering for the rest of the day. He was so easy to get along with I felt like I'd known him forever and could see why he was in the hospitality industry. He was high energy, flexible and fun to be with.

Despite still being unfinished, the Crazy Horse Memorial was to me the most impressive site on the trip. The monument was started by Korczak Ziolkowski in 1948 almost twenty years after a Lakota elder, Henry Standing Bear, had written to him to ask him to complete the work, saying in part, 'My fellow chiefs and I would like the white man to know that the red man has great heroes, too…'

The memorial receives no federal or state funding and is a non-profit undertaking, which may explain why it still isn't finished. Unfortunately Ziolkowski died in 1982, sixteen years before the face of Crazy Horse was completed and dedicated. The work is being carried on by Ziolkowski's wife, Ruth, and seven of their ten children!

I found myself really moved by the story and by the motto Ziolkowski lived by, *Never forget your dreams*. It struck a chord with me and with what I was doing and also reminded me of Adam.

Toby and I had lunch afterwards and I shared with him more about me and my trip than I normally did on my dates. He joined Sam and Max in knowing that I was dating someone in every state and writing a book about it.

'Better be on my best behaviour then,' he joked afterwards.

'Just be you, I like you better that way,' I remarked and we continued on our day.

In the evening before we parted company, Toby stopped before getting out of the car back at the Starbucks where we'd started.

'Meeeeelll,' he said, hesitantly.

'Yeeeas,' I replied, using his same lengthened phrasing.

'If you are dating someone in every state, how come we're driving together across the border into Montana and Wyoming tomorrow?'

'I'm cheating!' I laughed, then paused and corrected myself. 'It's fifty dates in fifty states, Tobes'. I cocked my head at him. 'Is tomorrow a date still?'

'Sure is from my side,' he replied with a grin.

'Then I'm still having a date in each state. It's just with the same guy for these three, that's all!'

'Well, that's OK, then,' he replied with a smile and a glint in his eye. 'But tomorrow I'm driving! We need something with a little more grunt than your rental car if we hit bad weather.'

'It's a deal!'

'And I'm bringing an extra thick jacket – you look like you've been freezing all day in that pathetic hoodie,' he said with a parting shot before shutting the car door.

The following day was even better than the first even if we were driving for what seemed like an eternity. It also reminded me of the marathon drive I had in front of me the next day for my return to Omaha, which I tried to put out of my mind.

I sat sideways in the front seat most of the day, facing Toby and happily yakking away as though catching up on the exploits of an old friend after years of being apart.

He occasionally pointed out of the window at something I was about to miss but I preferred the view of him in front of me. Eventually, he started pulling over and stopping so I would look at a distant mountain that he felt was particularly noteworthy.

At one point he got out of the car, marched around to my side, and with a bit of force pulled me out to gawk at the view. Already in his arms I stayed there and breathed into him. I knew what was going to happen next, and I was quite comfortable for it to occur, as I looked up, he cricked his neck to kiss me.

I liked Toby!

On my drive back to Omaha the next day, I mused about whether I could live in South Dakota. Dragging Toby out of a job he loved and his comfort zone, which I got the impression would be difficult for him to leave, was not on the cards as far as I could see.

This reality made me reflect on what I was wanting in a man. Having met so many, I was beginning to work it out.

Top of the list, I wanted someone fun who I could laugh with. I wanted a man I could be myself with and not have to put on airs and graces. I needed to be comfortable having a laugh and being my dorky self.

I wanted someone who could challenge me intellectually although they didn't need to have a high powered job – I again thought of Adam, who had an amazing brain but followed his own path. I wanted someone with that trait.

Having gone out with so many guys with no emotional intelligence whatsoever, I realised I needed this as well as a guy who made me feel secure. And not secure in that he was built like a tank but secure because he made me feel like the most important person in his life and would remind me every day of how much he loved me. Given my trust issues, this would be an important one.

I also wanted someone who was prepared to move for me rather than my always being the person who had to bend and change my life. A man who would stretch out of his comfort zone and try new things with me. I wanted a fellow adventurer.

It was quite a list and I noticed it was getting more specific as I was getting further along my journey.

I also noticed that not once had I placed any requirement on him being good-looking, having a certain hair-colour or being a certain height. None of that mattered anyway. I'd certainly discovered that along the way.

Later that night, in Omaha, Nebraska, in a horrible flea-ridden room in the worst hotel I stayed in during the whole trip, I wrote again to Adam.

Hello my gorgeous Adamski!

I've just had two great days, but then you probably know that if you're keeping an eye on me.

I know I haven't told you lately, but I miss you.

I'm having fun again, Adamski, but I'm struggling with something. I want so much in a man that I'm concerned I may be asking too much. And yet I don't want to settle.

That's always been my problem, hasn't it?! But I don't want an average life, playing wife and pretending to be happy – it just isn't me. If it were I'd still be married and have two kids by now.

Just the thought of it makes me shudder. And think of all the great experiences I would have missed out on. No working in Parliament House, no travelling the world, no climbing mountains in Nepal.

Do I really want a man if I'm making it so difficult for someone to live up to my expectations?

And I've been thinking about my running around like crazy on this military exercise I've been on since breaking up with Sam.

By giving myself such little time in each place, I think I made it impossible to meet someone and get to know them properly. Which begs the question again, do I really want to meet someone or have I just been going through the motions?

Writing to you now I realised that my barriers have been up ever since Sam. No one stood a chance, not even poor Toby, who is just a darling.

I was going to write more, but Max, the drummer from New Orleans called. Max had been the one guy who'd kept in touch all the way through with the occasional text or calls. I had enjoyed speaking with him over the couple of months since we'd met.

We had a chat and I realised I wanted to see him again since our time in New Orleans had been so brief.

'Max, I've been wondering if you fancy catching up again?'

'I'd love to,' he replied. 'Are you coming through New Orleans again?'

'Nope.' I hesitated a moment before saying, 'Ummm, I wondered if you wanted to come and meet me somewhere.'

'My schedule is pretty hectic, but I'll see what I can do. Where are you off to next?'

I walked him through my itinerary, which, in the next couple of weeks, was going to take in West Virginia, Ohio, Kentucky, Missouri, Kansas, Colorado, Hawaii and Mexico before a few days back in LA where I'd finally fly to New York and make my connection home to the UK.

'Bloody hell, you are covering some ground! I'd love to meet you in Mexico, but I'm not sure I can take that much time off. Let me check my schedule and flight costs etc. and get back to you in the new few days, OK?'

'No worries, it'd just be lovely to see you again,' I replied and with that I went to sleep.

A few days later, Max called as I was in Ohio driving to Kentucky.

'Mexico?' I asked as soon as I picked up the phone.

'No can do, I'm afraid, Mel. The flights now are really expensive and there's no way I can take that amount of time off.' He paused and then said, 'I can make a night in LA with you though if you'd like?'

I brightened. 'That'd be great, Max' I said.

'You book the flights and I'll book the hotel.'

We made some more plans, and I rang off.

Most of the men in these last few states were genuine, kind and true gentlemen. I did connect with a few, especially Tobes and Roberto but, maybe because I had now known Max for seven weeks or more, I felt I wanted to give him another shot.

And, obviously he thought I was worth the effort of flying up to LA! I decided I would book the hotel closer to the date so I could determine whether it would be one room or two. I have no doubt Max would have been thinking about and hoping for a sexual encounter the next time we met but I wanted to stay in control of the outcome – who knows who I could meet between now and then?!

Hawaii

I've been to the island of Oahu, Hawaii a number of times. In fact, it was where I surprised my ex-husband, Scott, back in 1998 as he arrived in Pearl Harbour on an Australian Naval ship.

I'd spoken to the sailors on the base and they'd let me in to stand on the dock as the shipped pulled in. That was before the Twin Towers attack, and I reflected that there would be no chance of my achieving this now no matter how sweetly I smiled at the guards.

As the ship pulled in, all the young sailors were lined up along the edge of the ship in true military fashion, stood to attention in their white uniforms they made quite a sight.

The ship docked and sailors were beginning to move and go back to their duties when I finally spotted Scott. When we eventually locked eyes, his face lit up and he beamed down at me. Large eyes gleaming with emotion and, with a big toothy grin on his round face he was the spitting image of a young Robin Williams.

It was a complete surprise to him as I'd left him in Australia, gone on to New Zealand and was supposed to be travelling around Asia at the time.

I smiled as I remembered the time we had together. I really had loved him. After eight years of not talking, he contacted me last year, saying he wanted to see me again, but also asked if he could see our dog, Jessie. When we met up, I got the impression he'd missed her far more than me as she got the bigger hug!

It had been good to see him again and we agreed to keep in touch as friends.

Thinking about Scott brought back many happy memories, however, I was pleased that my date here was not someone from my past but instead someone in my potential future.

Date #43: Jonny – Swimming With The Sharks

My date was an energetic and funny man called Jonny. He was in his early thirties and a native of Hawaii.

In person he was a sweetie, six-foot four and handsome with black hair. Writing this I have now seen him in his swimming gear and I can authoritatively say that he has a great body, which, through no fault of his, caused me to feel more than a little self-conscious in my bikini.

Our date was on the North of the Island of Oahu where we were going shark diving. It was his first time and, as we drove there together, he seemed pretty excited and a little nervous I think—unless he is always so chatty!

When he asked if I'd been shark diving before, I admitted that I had and actually in Hawaii. I'd chosen to do it again because although I'd enjoyed my first experience, I hadn't been able to fully experience it.

When I'd been, I'd entered the sea with no other equipment than my bikini – and a bloody big cage around me, obviously! Basically the metal cage floats with the aid of buoys that are attached to the top, which is open. It's kind of like jumping into a floating, open tin can but the walls of the can are made up of strong bars spaced far enough apart that you can get a good view but not enough for a shark to be able to get through and cause any harm.

When I went I had a problem with buoyancy. Despite my effort to stay down in the cage, I kept floating to the surface with my bottom inevitably leading the way, much to the amusement of the Japanese tourists who were on the boat taking photos.

Jonny cheekily said he'd stay in the boat with his camera if that was going to be the entertainment for the trip. Then, in all seriousness, he promised if I had issues, he would pull me down as he knew he sank like a stone.

We agreed to this tactic but I hoped I would not need any assistance as I had earlier contacted the company and ordered a weight-belt, the same type as used in diving. Having dived before, I knew that a weight-belt laden with metal bars would prevent me floating so readily to the surface.

Luckily, it worked a treat and I stayed down much longer only needing to surface a couple of times with the correct part of my anatomy leading the way as I came up and gasped in big lung fulls of air before heading back down.

Having seen the movie *Jaws* when I was about 4 years old, I remember being terrified in my living room watching as the shark circled and attacked. I have been petrified of sharks ever since. However, I have to admit they're amazing creatures. Built for exactly what they need to do, they are sleek, powerful and completely terrifying when they approach the cage from the murky depths and whip it with their tail or body as they circle attracted by the blood from the entrails of meat that the men in the boat throw in once you have safely jumped into the cage and entered the water.

I didn't think about it last time, but it was pretty disgusting to be swimming in the middle of a whole heap of bloody entrails and meat from goodness knows what kind of animal.

Safe in the bottom of the cage this time, it was really an exhilarating experience to be so near them in their environment, without having to worry about my bottom floating to the surface or my fingers being wrapped around the metal bars as I tried to stay put.

Jonny loved it, too, and, given the adrenaline, was even chattier on the way back. He seemed really pleased that he'd thrown caution to the wind and both met me for the date and gone along with my idea to shark dive.

I had a really great time with him, so much so that I forgot completely to brush my hair after the dive. With that and the car windows down, by the time I got back to the hotel, I looked like I had been dragged through a hedge backwards.

I didn't realise this, however, until after I'd said good-bye to Jonny and caught a glimpse of myself in reception and saw, to my horror, that my hair was sticking out at all angles. On closer examination I noticed that my face was also pink and freckly and I looked like an older version of Pippi Longstocking!

It obviously hadn't bothered Jonny, who had kissed me goodbye and asked if I wanted to have dinner as well. There was an awkward moment when I had a feeling that dinner wasn't the only thing he wanted.

After all of the excitement of the day, the mad dash to Hawaii, not to mention having covered so many other US states in such a short time, all I actually wanted was to go to bed early, and alone, before getting back on a plane the next day. So I did the adult thing and politely declined.

Mexico

By the time I got to Mexico a day and a bit later, I was physically and emotionally exhausted.

Travelling from state to state with no break was just plain tiring and making the crazy dash to Hawaii for three days had finally done me in.

I'd been doing everything at warp speed, including eating, and, except during lunch or dinner dates, had consumed fast food pretty much every day. It was an easy, but not healthy, diet and my body now craved fruit and vegetables.

I was also looking forward to sleeping until noon and not knowing what day it was.

My last few weeks really had been like a military operation, and I'd had to organise all of the logistics including flight, rental cars, hotels, driving routes, and dates for each state as well. This in itself was sufficient to make me tired, but on each new date I was always trying to think of questions and topics to talk about to put my date and me at ease. After a while it felt like a drag and was mentally taxing.

I'd now been through forty-one states and Washington D.C. and dated more than fifty men. (I doubled up in a few states because I hadn't been able to choose just one eligible guy when there were so many!)

I'd enjoyed my trip so far but desperately wanted and needed time in one place. I now had a week in Mexico, the thought of which was heaven.

Hawaii had put me in the mood for lying by the pool in the sunshine as the weather there had been a welcome change from the rest of mainland America, which was now definitely getting colder as we headed towards winter in the northern hemisphere. I had already endured the Australian winter back in June, July and August and was quite happy to postpone entering the season for the second time this year.

My hotel in the small town of La Paz in Baja Sur, Mexico had a pool with a view over the ocean and a small private beach. It wasn't a five-star resort but it was definitely one of the better hotels I'd seen as I travelled through the small town in the taxi ride from the airport.

There was a dive school onsite that also took people on snorkel trips with the whale sharks. Having thoroughly enjoyed the shark experience with Jonny, I decided this was a must for the end of the trip. And this time no cage, as I would be swimming with whale sharks who, although apparently the size of a bus, were harmless. For now though, all I wanted to do was sleep by the pool, read and swim.

I swam and slept and swam and slept and realised that I was still really cut up over Sam. Having learnt the lesson to let myself experience my emotions, I allowed myself time to wallow in grief as I thought about him.

Despite our only having been together for a short time, I really missed him. It'd been so wonderful to connect with someone in such a close way and I thought again of how difficult it was to find that kind of connection.

By day four, I was beginning to feel not only more refreshed but more toned as well from all of the swimming. I found that when I swam, my brain had the freedom to process what I'd been through and what I still wanted. After swimming, I felt calm and clear.

After the counselling session, which had opened my eyes to how the brain works, I'd read more about the subject. Initially it was because I needed more evidence to allow me to feel okay with my reaction. However, even after I'd forgiven myself, I still continued to read. I was fascinated by how the brain works and how we process emotions and events.

I had known that allowing the brain time at rest, usually during exercise, provided the right environment for it to process and take in new information. Even armed with that knowledge over the past few years, I had not allowed myself this luxury. In fact, after Adam died I stopped exercising altogether and even my dog walks were much shorter.

I wondered if at some level I had done this on purpose. I hadn't wanted to believe Adam was dead so I had given myself very little time to process that this was indeed a fact. However, my mind used my time asleep to try to process his death, and I had many dreams about it.

I lay on the sun bed by the pool and closed my eyes, thinking of all that Adam had meant to me, as a partner, friend and soul mate. The pain of that loss still felt very real and much greater in comparison to my loss of Sam. It put that relationship into perspective.

I also realised that under the surface I had been stressing about how I would feel and what would happen if I didn't meet my Mr. Right on this trip.

After agreeing to write a book about my travels, I had subconsciously felt under pressure to provide not only myself but everyone else the happy ending we all want in life.

'Sorry,' I muttered to the people to whom I had sold my book. 'I will deliver on the book, but I can't promise the happy ending.'

The cynic in me found a voice as I reflected that if I returned home single then my book would at least reflect the realities of life—not everyone gets a happy ending. And with that, I tried to shrug off the burden I had imposed on myself.

So what if I didn't find Mr. Right? I had met so many wonderful people that had added value to my life in various ways that they would probably never know. I'd seen almost all of the states and would visit the rest after Christmas.

I was having fun and had learned so much about myself in such a short time that I decided that was enough.

With that, I breathed a huge sigh of relief. I liked my own company. I was happy and content and had great friends back in the UK, Australia and now the US. If I weren't meant to find a new partner, so be it. I had my health, wonderful friends, great work connections and could easily support myself. My life was good. I didn't need Mr. Right to complete me.

Later that evening I ran into Matt, who was staying at the hotel and diving at the school. We'd spoken a couple of times at the pool and hotel bar. He was in his early twenties and a serious young fellow who was just getting into his career in New York City. He asked if I'd like to join him and another young lad for dinner. Feeling refreshed after my self-imposed isolation, I agreed.

We went to a local bar and restaurant that his friend, Joel had chosen. As we walked up the winding stairs that reminded me of the old stone steps in church towers, I looked up and saw a handsome face with bright blue eyes staring back at me from the top of the stairs. I smiled and walked past him with Matt to the dining area where Joel joined us.

We had a delicious meal and a few cocktails and chatted easily about travel, diving and other adventure sports. Joel, like me, was an outdoors type who liked an adrenaline rush or two.

When the lads suggested we go back to the bar area, I readily agreed as I'd noticed the handsome guy with the blue sparkly eyes was still there and still looking at me. I sat with Matt and Nathan nearly across from him and, when he caught my eye, smiled back at him.

After several more cocktails the inevitable happened. I needed the bathroom, which was next to the table where the handsome man was sitting with his friend. I noticed that he didn't look Mexican but didn't look American either. Maybe European, I mused.

When I came out of the bathroom I looked at him. He met my eye and then nodded to his table where I saw three tequilas. One in front of him, one in front of his friend and one slightly off to the side. He looked at me again and then back at the tequila and wordlessly invited me to join the two of them.

The two young lads had been perfectly oblivious to the silent conversation that I'd been having for around an hour with this man, so they must have been surprised when I grabbed my bag, said, 'Excuse me,' and walked to his table.

José introduced himself in Spanish and I said hello in English. His friend turned out to be a new work colleague, Carlos, who knew a little English, which was more than José did.

Already well on my way to being drunk when I joined him for the tequila, the rest of the night was spent downing shots and laughing as we tried to understand what the other was saying whilst Carlos tried to keep up and translate.

José was from Spain and had only arrived in La Paz the day before to start work on an engineering project in the area. I noticed that his twinkly eyes, which had appeared blue in the distance, now seemed greenie brown. He had a cheeky smile which was endearing despite his not having the gleaming white teeth I had become accustomed to in America.

He was definitely handsome with a slim build and the traditional dark brown hair, thick eyebrows and light olive skin that most Mediterranean men seem to have. He wore his hair slightly longer than normal and the shaggy look gave the impression of someone with a free spirit.

Despite not understanding him I could tell that he was confident and charismatic as the two waitresses that were taking it in turns to serve us were clearly flirting with him while dropping off each fresh round of tequila or mescal (smoked tequila and thus more potent), which I'd challenged him to try.

We had a great time together and were amongst the last patrons at the bar. Matt and Nathan had left earlier and I'd assured them in the confident manner of someone who had consumed too much alcohol that I'd be fine. However, when I looked around I began to panic about how the hell I was going to get back to the hotel.

José must have noticed my change of mood and put his hand reassuringly on my arm. He pointed at himself then motioned like he was driving a car and pointed at me and said the word hotel. I smiled and nodded and said thank you.

When I sobered up the next day, I realised that had been foolish after consuming so much alcohol. Thankfully, he managed to drive without incident and after a peck on the cheek goodnight asked through various gestures if he could take me to the beach the next day. I nodded and we pointed at our watches to organise a time.

The next morning I woke up several times with a terrible thumping headache and kept turning over to sleep some more in the hope it would go away. I ventured down to the dining area around 1 p.m. and opted for the plainest thing on the menu, which was a chicken sandwich. When it arrived I took one bite and realised I still wasn't up for eating —that mescal had been lethal.

I took the chicken sandwich and retreated to my room with a niggling feeling I'd organised something for later in the day. Despite it hurting to do so, I tried to think, and the events of the night came into focus.

Back in my room I rummaged in my bag for my camera. I looked at the two photos from the evening's shenanigans. Yes, he appeared real... I had managed to bag myself a date with a seriously hot Spaniard!

I looked at my watch and saw that I had fewer than two hours before he was coming to pick me up. I forced myself to have a couple more mouthfuls of the chicken sandwich and set my alarm for an hour later. I decided more sleep was the best course of action to try and make myself look presentable later.

Date #44: José – My Unofficial Date

When José arrived with Carlos in tow, it occurred to me that maybe this wasn't a date after all. This feeling intensified as Carlos chatted to me while José drove in silence.

By the time we arrived at the beach I had made up my mind that this was definitely not a date, just two nice gents who'd decided to treat a tourist to an afternoon swim. With that in my mind, I happily stripped to my bikini. I didn't need to be self-conscious around two men who clearly had no interest in any romantic kind of liaison with me.

On the beach blanket, Carlos continued to talk and I noticed José getting more withdrawn. I tapped his arm and pointed to the water and the two of us. His face lit up and he nodded in agreement. As we waded out he grabbed my hand and smiled at me. I was a little surprised but smiled back.

The water was pretty shallow so we needed to wade a fair distance before being able to swim. Carlos decided to join us. José spotted him in the distance and suddenly looked annoyed.

He quickly motioned to me that he wanted us to have a meal together and I nodded eagerly. He nodded in Carlos' direction, looked back at me and shook his head. I got the message he wanted it to be just the two of us. My smile widened as I indicated that from my point of view this was perfect.

When Carlos arrived, José looked across at me like a fellow conspirator and then possessively put his arm around me to demonstrate very clearly to Carlos that, despite the language barrier, I was with him. I couldn't help but smile to myself as it dawned on me that he was, indeed, a hot-blooded Mediterranean man who liked me.

Later that night he took me out for a meal. Despite his only knowing two English words when we first met, 'hello' and 'yesterday' (and he didn't actually know what yesterday meant, he just hummed the Beatles song each time he said it), we got on fabulously.

Without the need for any common language we just clicked and giggled like amused children as we struggled to communicate with hand, body and facial gestures. And also like children, we began to learn a little of the other's language.

The following day we got together again. Armed with pen and notebook, we went to another beach, just the two of us. The day seemed to fly by and neither of us had wanted to say good-bye at the end of the night.

José had to work the next day and he now knew this would also be my last day in Mexico. We had one final dinner together and he asked me if he could stay the night. Wanting to spend as much time with him as possible, I agreed.

I hadn't spent the night wrapped in anyone's arms since leaving Sam and laid with José as he held me gave me a calm, safe feeling again.

Waking up was not quite as wonderful as another typical Mel moment occurred. Around 6 a.m. I woke myself up with a loud fart. I know it happens to everyone at one time or another, and it startled me so much that I couldn't help but giggle. Not remembering José was in bed with me, I tittered slightly and then froze.

I realised José was behind me and would have received the full force of the wind that had emanated from my bottom. I closed my eyes tightly and prayed to the universe that he was still fast asleep. Unbeknown to me at the time José was wide awake and also trying to remain perfectly still in an effort not to shudder with laughter. He pretended to stir a few minutes later and indicated to me that he needed to go to work.

Mortified, I was suddenly very relieved and pleased to be leaving later that morning and despite it being José's first full week on the new project, he sneaked out of work to take me to the airport and say goodbye.

With the memory of the morning's incident in bed still fresh in my mind, I didn't spend as much time as I wanted to hugging and kissing José good-bye. I still had a desire to simply hide and cringe at yet another humiliating experience in my life.

Plus, despite our having exchanged email addresses, if I'm honest, I didn't really expect to hear from him again.

When I arrived in LA I tried to put José from my mind and reminded myself that I was meeting Max for the short time I was there. I had a few hours to kill before his plane was due, so I picked up the rental car I'd organised and headed to a suburb a few miles away. Finding my usual source of free wifi, I settled into a seat at Starbucks with a mocha and slice of lemon cake.

I opened my email and found that in the few hours since I'd left Mexico, José had emailed me three times. I smiled and tried to read through the emails but had no idea what he was saying. It was all in Spanish.

I emailed him back in English, thanking him for a truly amazing time and was surprised when he replied straight away with the words *I miss you*, in English. His friend Carlos had obviously helped him with that!

Feeling a little trepidation now, I picked Max up from the airport late in the afternoon. We went to Santa Monica for a stroll on the pier as he bombarded me with questions about my trip to this point.

When we got to the end of the pier I leaned on the wooden rail to look at the view. I was not surprised when standing on the pier looking out to sea, Max, who was behind me, wrapped me in his arms. When I'd set up these couple of days, it was clear at the time that both of us were hoping for a romantic encounter.

I felt guilty as my skin recoiled at his touch and an image of José appeared in my head. Max was still Max and nothing for him had changed, but I realised I now felt completely differently.

When he turned me around to kiss me, I didn't stop him but neither did I kiss him back. I looked at him and realised no matter how awkward it was I was going to have to tell him. I pulled away from his embrace and started walking back towards the beach. And, not looking in his direction but aware of his presence next to me, started to tell him how I was feeling.

'I'm so sorry,' I exclaimed. 'I know you have just spent money and your time to meet up with me again, but I am feeling really weird about this. I've met someone and, although it may go nowhere, I'm feeling incredibly ashamed and guilty at being with you.'

I told him about José and Mexico. Max was clearly disappointed but accepted it as the gentleman he is. He asked if we could still spend the time together and I said I'd love that if he was still happy to be my friend.

Initially it was a little awkward, especially as we got to the hotel and the lady at reception clearly thought we would be taking one room not two. But, when it came time for both of us to leave, I was pleased I'd seen Max again and was happy at our new friendship.

Also, being in Sam's neck of the woods, I couldn't help but think of him, especially when I nipped to Lorence's to pick up my other suitcase. I remembered our drive back when he'd admitted he didn't feel the same way about me as I did about him.

The memory of it still stung, but I could now see that if that was the way he felt, he'd done the right thing. Even though I had wished things had been different, I couldn't make him love me.

It was what it was and Sam was a decent, honourable man who would make someone extremely happy one day... it just wouldn't be me.

A couple of days later, on the plane back to the UK, I closed my eyes and escaped into my own little world. What a journey it had been!

My life had changed so much this year already. Emerging from exhaustion and living in a work-crazed, hypertensive state I had remembered my Positive Change Formula and had successfully worked through the first six steps.

I was proud that I had stuck to my plan and was relieved that I only had another nine states to go. I wasn't sure where things were going with José, who was still emailing me in Spanish several times a day, but was enjoying the attention and anticipation of opening my computer to see whether he had contacted me or not – which invariably he had.

I decided in the UK I would look on the internet and find a site that could translate his messages. I desperately wanted to know what he was saying. But again, without the need to understand his words, I understood his actions. He seriously liked me and was missing me. I smiled at the memory of him and realised I was missing him too.

And then my thoughts turned to the UK. Growing serious, I swallowed hard as I thought about what I wanted to say to my parents. How would I explain that I had been date-raped at sixteen and never told them, and more importantly why I hadn't said a word.

I wasn't sure what would hurt them more. Telling them I had been raped or telling them that I had not felt safe enough with them at the time to admit to them what had happened.

I knew now, in the years that had passed that they had tried their best with me as I had been growing up. However, when I was younger I saw things very differently. I always felt like a stranger looking in at the family rather than feeling like I was a member of it.

After various incidents growing up, that view was further reinforced and I felt very alone and unable to share anything with either my parents or my sister.

I had a difficult relationship with both my parents who struggled to deal with a curious, bright and strong-willed daughter whose interests and personality was very different to their own.

The image of my mum floated before my eyes. We shared the same features, her nose, mouth, eyes and facial structure were all mine. The only difference was she had dark skin and black hair whilst I possessed the colouring from dad's side of the family—pale skin and the exact same red hair as my Uncle Malc.

However, throughout the majority of my life we had shared little else. I realised it had only been in the last couple of years that I had really got to know my mum. She had overcome her own setbacks, the death of her mother at fifteen, a difficult father and she had sacrificed a career as a teacher to marry my dad and have me and Nic.

She had obviously struggled with her own demons growing up and it had taken her longer to come to terms with them and set them aside than it had for me. Consequently, we had endured a difficult relationship for many years and for several had not talked to each other at all.

However, I felt after learning more about her, that my mum deserved a second chance and I wanted to get to know her better. How I was going to do that was still not clear in my mind, although I knew it would involve some honest conversations.

And then I thought of my dad, who was going to pick me up at the airport. I smiled.

Dad and I had shared a real bond when I was young. I was a tomboy and the son he wanted. Up until my early teens we would wrestle and play cowboys together and I would help him when he ventured into the garden, invariably to saw or destroy something. My dad loved chopping trees down and I had loved the deep growl of the chainsaw as the wood succumbed to it.

However, our relationship had become strained and distant once I truly entered my teenage years. Whether it was because he found living with teenage girls difficult or because he and my mum were growing apart, or because he wanted so much to build a successful business I am not entirely sure but he spent less time at home and more and more hours at work.

The only time I really got to spend with him for the last few years before I left for university was on a Saturday morning when I would join him in his real estate business and help out on the front counter.

I sighed nostalgically.

I really hoped he would give me a chance and get to know me as an adult now rather than remembering me only as the difficult teenager I was, the memories of which were obviously still front and centre in his mind, given the comments he made over the phone sometimes.

I knew my dad and I would never be as close as we were when I was a child but I hoped we could rekindle some of that and more importantly he would accept me for the adult I had become.

Back in the UK with my family

As the plane started its descent I realised that I would find out soon enough if I could forge a bond again with my parents—I was almost back in the UK.

When I landed in England it was a freezing cold, grey day and it was chucking it down with rain.

'Typical,' I said to no one in particular as I looked out at Manchester Airport through the plane window letting out an involuntarily shudder.

My dad stood in the arrivals hall looking for me when I strode confidently through the thick automatic doors that swung open at my approach. He gave me a big hug asking, 'How are you then, monkey?' probably much to his regret as I spent the next hour and a half on the way home happily regaling him with details of my trip.

That happiness and excitement soon dissipated in the days that followed. Although it was wonderful to make the rounds and see each of my family members again after such a long time I realised that I still felt a huge distance between us even though I was sat across from them. With sadness I noticed I had been more at ease with perfect strangers on my travels.

In a short time after stepping back on English soil my mood and my health spiralled downwards at a rapid rate. The icy wind bit and tore at my hands and face, whatever skin was not fully covered turned red and then blue in the cold. I felt frozen to the core both from the weather and the company.

However, when I visited my Aunty Barb and her daughter, Deb I would thaw, inside and out.

Sitting in Deb's conservatory despite the cold, we huddled together conspiratorially, giggling and chattering merrily.

'Let's see some photos then,' she urged prodding me and pointing at my iPad sitting on the table. 'I know there are photos in that thing, and I want to see them!'

Deb, a few years older than me, is more like a big sister in many respects than a cousin. In fact, since we look a little alike, we've often been asked if this is the case.

She is shorter than I am, however, and her hair tends to fluctuate between dark brown and blonde depending on the time of year and what mood she's in. She's worn glasses ever since I can remember but they suit her and I cannot imagine her face without them.

She settled down with her husband, Dave, years before and has three wonderful young lads. Even though years can pass between visits, the boys all give fabulous hugs whenever they see me.

Deb and I shared a number of exploits when we were younger, some of which we even managed to get away with. And she, together with her mum, my Aunty Barb, had been the two people I felt most comfortable being myself around. They never judged me and so when I spoke to them I was generally more open about how I was feeling.

After I had shown Deb shots of various places in America, she piped up, 'Yes, Meg, but where are the photos of your dates?'

I admitted that after getting photos of, or with, the first couple of dates, I'd noticed it had given them the wrong impression. They'd either happily thought I was more serious than I was or appeared concerned about it.

'So, in the end,' I confessed, 'I just got them to take photos of me.'

'So, who are these two then?' She pointed towards small images she could see of Sam and José when I'd gone back to scan mode.

'That one...' I said pointing to Sam on the screen which made him appear in full focus, '...broke my heart'. Deb took in his face, 'No great loss' she noted.

'And that one...' I said, bringing José's picture up so it filled the screen. 'That one... 'I'm still not sure about.'

I told Deb all about our adventures together in Mexico and that he'd emailed me every day since I'd left.

She said, 'Hell, good-looking and a sweetheart! What are you messing at Meg? Get talking to him on Skype. He obviously likes you, and from what you say you like him too.'

Realising the truth of this statement I got José's Skype address later that night and we began to chat. It was more of a struggle trying to talk via computer, but when we both discovered Google translate (which allows you to type in whole sentences in one language and will then translate it into the other) things got easier.

We Skyped most days and it turned out to be the highlight of many as I became sick with what was diagnosed as a chest infection but was in fact pneumonia.

After my first week back, Georgia my best mate in Australia was aghast when she saw the change in me and as I broke down in tears whilst talking to her, her concern was touching as she almost pleaded with me to return to Australia. 'Come back, Mel' she urged. 'Clearly England is no good for you.'

I was sorely tempted to flee, feeling and probably behaving as I had done in my teenage years, which was exactly what I had wanted *not* to happen.

'I promised I'd have Christmas with my folks,' I said, downcast and sullen. 'I'll survive. But can we Skype a little more whilst I am here?'

'Always got time for you.' she said brightly and I smiled thankful for having such a loyal friend.

Unable and unwilling to venture far from the house in the next few weeks I retreated to my bedroom and when I had the house to myself could be found curled up on the sofa in front of the fire glued to my computer.

I idled away the time between Skype conversations with either Miss G or José by escaping into my memories and creating a playlist to remind me of each of the states I'd visited. Some referenced the states themselves, some the men and some simply reflected my mood at the time. Retreating into my own world as I had as a child, I realised at once that I had reverted back to old behaviours and determined that once I felt better I would talk to my parents and reassert my adult self.

In the meantime, I would curl up and look forward to speaking with José.

One evening just before Christmas when I was trying and failing to converse fluidly with José, much to my surprise my dad's voice piped up behind me as he leaned over my shoulder looking at José's image on the computer screen and started addressing him... in Spanish.

I looked at my dad incredulously and he laughed at me and clearly told José that I didn't know he could speak Spanish. They appeared to have an animated conversation and I felt a little bit like a spare wheel. After that, Dad took to shouting *Hola* at José when I picked up his Skype calls and skittered nervously out of the room eager to talk to him myself.

With the aid of Google translate we were now learning far more about each other and one evening he nervously confided in me that he had a daughter – and a wife whom he was separated from.

'Are you divorced yet?' I typed and sat back taking a sharp intake of breathe as I nervously awaited the answer. 'No.' Came the reply and my face must have betrayed my disappointment as José responded by calling my name and urging me to look at the computer and thus him.

We discussed the subject some more and I tried not to judge him for the actions of my ex-fiancé, Kyle. Not every separated man was a lying cheat.

Ok. I thought, as it seems the time that we are sharing secrets I had better tell him mine. 'I've been dating fifty men in fifty states,' I wrote and looked up to see his reaction. He looked at me and again at the translated message clearly concerned and confused. The inevitable question was raised and I replied that, 'No, I had not had sex with them all. It was simply a first date with each.' He seemed relieved until I typed, 'I have nine states left.'

That did not go down well, especially when I explained that I intended to go back to the US in January and complete the dates. 'If you are going back to the US, you must come first to Mexico so I can persuade you to stay with me' was his reply. I looked up and into the computer screen grinning into his serious face and nodded excitedly. Yes, I would love that.

Agreeing to head back in the New Year by the next morning I had my flights booked – I would be arriving back in La Paz, Mexico on the 3rd of January 2012.

Happier now with this to look forward to I pushed to the back of my mind that I still needed to work on my relationship with my parents which had not improved dramatically since I had arrived. In fact, I think my hibernating in the house had only reinforced my dad's view that I hadn't changed much since my teenage years.

Still sick, when I left, I decided that I would come back in the UK summer and try again. But for now I didn't have the strength to have those hard conversations. Instead for my final days with them over the Christmas season I simply tried to make the most of the family events and the short time I now had before leaving again for Mexico.

CHAPTER 8

Victory

Mexico again... and 8 of the 9 states

*W*hen José met me at the airport I admit I was nervous about seeing him again. It was all very well talking on Skype but, for the next two weeks, I would be living with him in the apartment he shared with his friend and work mate, Raul.

However, I had an escape plan. If José and I didn't get on, I would head back to the hotel I was at when we first met until I needed to leave. It was just a two weeks out of my life and no big deal.

But as I arrived and caught a glimpse of him standing nervously in the arrivals hall I hoped I wouldn't need to leave. His skin now darker from more exposure to the sun, he looked like a model.

He met me with a wide smile and a kiss, which I spotted as I peeked through half-closed eyes, was being met with a jealous looks on the faces of a number of ladies in the airport who had also taken notice of this handsome man.

When I got to his apartment I saw a host of green and blue sticky notes scattered around the house and stuck on various objects. On closer inspection I noticed written on each was the name of the object in English. I was touched to see that José had been busy trying to learn the language so we could communicate better. He was clearly serious about having a relationship with me, which gave me a warm feeling inside.

The next two weeks were idyllic. When José got home each night from work we would stroll down to the beach and along the promenade to watch the sun set. After which we'd duck into a local restaurant to sample their fare.

My Spanish was getting slightly better and so was his English and, although both of us got frustrated at times and there was some confusion when things got misinterpreted, we muddled through.

The two weeks flew by and both José and I were taken by surprise when we realised I had to leave in a couple of days. When I advised José that I was leaving his movements became like staccato music, short, crisp, detached. He nervously flitted around me jabbering in Spanish that I *had* to come back and that he wasn't ready for me to leave, not yet, not ever.

When I realised what he was saying I hugged him, my words and tone soothing. I wanted to come back too, and would if he would have me. He made me feel loved and secure. Not through his doting behaviour as he ran around wanting to make sure everything was perfect for me, even scolding waiters when we went out at night for not giving me the service he believed I deserved. Being doted on to such an extent was a novelty but I knew it wouldn't last.

It was in the small daily actions that he conveyed his feelings. Kissing me gently on the forehead every morning, he'd retreat to the bathroom to get ready for work, so he wouldn't disturb my slumber. And, if he saw women giving him admiring glances he wouldn't point them out but instead just reach across and subtly brush away a hair on my face or put his hand on my arm protectively to signal that he was with me.

So, when it came time to leave, I had no hesitation in agreeing to José's slightly petulant petitions that I leave clothes at his in a gesture of good faith that I'd return. His behaviour, though slightly demanding, made me feel loved and wanted as it signified his desperate desire to see me again – very different from Sam's actions.

New Hampshire, Vermont, Maine, Massachusetts, Rhode Island, Connecticut, Oregon, Washington

When I left it was to cover eight out of nine of my final states, although I only actually had three dates.

Charlie, whom I'd been speaking with over the internet before I met José, was going to show me New England: New Hampshire, Vermont, Maine, Massachusetts, Rhode Island and Connecticut to be exact.

Needless to say, when I boarded the plane, José was extremely agitated and unsettled by the fact that I was leaving to spend time with other men. And I too was feeling conflicted.

I still wasn't entirely sure how things would work out with José but I knew that any relationship with him was not going to be easy. On top of the language problems, José was also going through a messy divorce and had a young daughter who he loved and missed terribly. The reality of having a relationship with a man with so much baggage and the difficulties they presented were already evident after just two weeks of being together. I had to ask myself, 'Was he worth it?'

Dates #45-50: Charlie – Charlie And
The Hot Chocolate Factories of New England

When I finally met Charlie he was just as lovely in person as over the internet. Laid back, easy to talk to, tall, dirty blond hair, accomplished. He really was the whole package. But despite that we didn't make a deep connection. It's hard to explain why I just clicked with some people and not others and whilst he was easy to be with there was no 'click' for me.

We still had a great time together, driving through the New England countryside, stopping for hot chocolates and cosy lunches, but I found I was missing José. After a while I noticed what was different about being with Charlie and being with José.

With both I used my techniques to match and mirror them to make them feel more relaxed, but I realised that José, whether consciously or not, returned these gestures. It was all very well my doing what I could to make the other person feel comfortable and free to chat easily; however, there comes a time when I want someone to do that for me too.

That was the secret ingredient. José made me feel just as secure and relaxed as I made him. And he was genuinely interested and intrigued by me.

With this aha moment I wanted to get on a plane back to Mexico. However, I still had a commitment to keep so instead, after saying goodbye to Charlie, I boarded a plane to the other side of the US to meet my last two dates in Oregon and Washington.

Dates #51&52: Harry And Ian – I Left My Heart In...

I tried to be fully present and open to my next two dates, but my mind and heart were elsewhere. I found that I just wanted to get through them, enjoy catching up with new friends at the Loral Langemeier event I had signed up for when I knew I would be back in the US, and then get back to José as quickly as possible. I organised to fly back to him the day after the conference ended.

When I arrived back into La Paz airport, only two weeks after I had left, José met me with a huge smile that I am sure I mirrored without having to think about it because every time I see him he makes me smile.

He enveloped me in a warm hug, and then told me very sternly that I was not allowed to go away for so long again... and definitely no more dating other people.

'If you don't, I won't', I replied flippantly and, with that, we were a couple.

No matter what language barrier lay between us, José and I decided there and then that we would do our best to break it down. We spoke to each other partly in Spanish, partly in French, partly in English and the rest through body language and gestures. And even though we didn't understand everything the other said, José made me feel as though he really saw me like no one else did: my hopes, dreams, fallibilities and vulnerabilities. He accepted them and he accepted me.

A few weeks later it was Valentine's Day and, not having celebrated this particular 'holiday' for years, I was getting a bit nervous about what I should do and what was expected of me. I decided to go with understated... big mistake!

I bought a photo frame, printed some photos of the two of us to put inside and left it at that. However, when I returned home from the Spanish classes I was taking, I found José had taken advantage of my being out and nipped back to the house from his work to decorate the bed with glitter which surrounded a bottle of vintage Dom Perignon champagne he left on the pillow.

Shit! Now I had to step it up! I rushed out and bought some cheesy wrapping paper decorated with hearts and roses and sticky tape and scissors. I also found chocolates and a helium balloon with a message of love on it. Then I got to work.

I put the photo frame with the photos of the two of us on the wall, surrounded it with the hearts and flowers I cut from the wrapping paper and added to the wall the glitter that José had left on the bed. I placed the chocolates next to the champagne on the bed and tied the helium balloon to the champagne bottle.

There! He was not going to outdo me this time!

When he returned home from work, I was waiting for him in the bedroom. He walked in and stepped back as the decorated wall hit him full force. He grabbed me and danced around the small room hugging and kissing me as he swung me around.

As he examined the photos in the frame, I sat on the bed feeling thoroughly pleased with myself and had a warm glow inside, looking at José's happy face. It had only been four months since we first met but I didn't think I ever wanted to stop looking at him.

Then, he completely broke the mood. He tried to talk to me about work. He told me he had some papers he didn't understand that he wanted me to translate for him.

'Give them to Raul,' I said. With only ten hours of Spanish lessons behind me, I didn't quite feel up to translation work just yet.

José looked put out, sticking his bottom lip out as he grabbed the bundle of documents.

'No. You. You,' he said insistently and forced the pile of documents into my hands.

As I took the pile from him, a box fell out. I leant down to pick it up and looked at him. He gestured for me to open it and inside I saw a brightly cut diamond gleaming as it sat clasped on top of a bevelled edged yellow gold eighteen carat ring. It looked expensive and I glanced from it up at him a look of concern crossing my face.

Although I knew what it had to mean, I was a little confused. I noticed José was no longer looking relaxed, but a little bit panicked now.

Things were beginning to get awkward and I wasn't sure what to do. My stomach started to churn and my palms got sweaty as I knew I had to break the silence that had settled around us.

Nervously, I gestured with the ring between my left and right hands, and asked, 'What finger do you want me to put this on exactly?' I was stalling for time to sort through my feelings and also wanting to be clear what he was suggesting. I realised I was actually hoping it was what it appeared to be but didn't want to misconstrue his actions. Maybe he just had a lot of money and bought this as a generous gift?

He gestured to the Valentines card he'd left on the bed, which I had to admit I hadn't opened because I'd rushed out to get more romantic supplies when I'd seen the champagne.

I opened the card, saw that he had unsurprisingly written to me in Spanish and feeling very self conscious, I reached for the English/Spanish dictionary that was sat on the bedside table.

My body temperature rising, I felt myself become red, sweaty and nervous as I began to translate. The translation read, *My Mel, I love you. Would you like to spend the rest of your life with me? Your José.*

With a deep breath I took in the message. A multitude of emotions and thoughts rushed through me in quick succession—it's too soon!

You hardly know him! Are you sure? It's a huge risk! Do you love him already?

I settled firmly on the one emotion and thought that resonated and stuck. Yes, it was a risk. But if I got my heart broken down the track at least I'd tried and not run away. I was falling in love with this man and I wanted to be with him.

It had been a long and hard road to get here. Loving and losing Adam, my ex-husband Scott, my ex-fiancé Kyle, and then Sam.

I had doubted whether I was capable of loving someone again or of allowing myself to be loved. In meeting Sam, I realised that yes, I could do it again though he wasn't the right man.

Keeping any emotion from my face, I stared at José and took a deep, cleansing breath, again letting go of the past and saying goodbye to all my demons and the baggage I had been carrying around with me.

José, was standing absolutely still, he looked frozen in panic as he waited for my answer. My eyes locked with his and I smiled. No words were necessary.

He reached for my hand and pulled me up towards him.

'Yes?' he asked, quietly.

Calmly and seriously, I replied, 'Yes' and smiled contentedly as he took my face in his hands and smothered me with kisses.

And so, the English girl, living in Australia, looking for love in America, found a Spaniard in Mexico.

On that sunbed at the hotel in La Paz on my first visit to Mexico, I had finally let go of the hurt and pain of losing first Adam and then Sam. It was there I realised I was quite happy with who I was and where I was in my life.

Even though I hadn't realised it at the time, as soon as I was ready to allow him in, the universe almost immediately presented me with a new partner.

And, as the cynic in me wondered how long it would last, I realised I didn't care. Yes, I wanted it to last forever, but if it didn't at least I would have no regrets. I realised that it was only my inaction that I ever regretted and never my action—no matter how crazy. I wanted no more regrets in my life and I knew that if I didn't take this risk with José now that I would regret it forever and always be left wondering.

Shortly after we got engaged and moved into our own apartment, Ralph and Lauren joined us. José heard about a Labrador who had given birth to ten puppies. As she was unable to feed all of them the owners were looking to find people to take them, otherwise some faced a very short life.

José and I couldn't let that happen and even though we knew we would have to get them out of the country and jump through all the red tape necessary to do so, we were happy to take on the task.

The puppies were only two weeks old when we got them and tiny balls of energetic fur. Very quickly they developed their own little personalities and very quickly they doubled and tripled in size.

As soon as they were allowed to get wet they came kayaking with us. Lauren, standing at the front of the kayak, wind whipping her ears back thoroughly enjoyed the whole experience. Standing there, she reminded me of Rose in the scene on the movie the Titanic, where she stands at the front of the ship, arms open wide thrilled by the view of the open ocean in front of her.

From her perch Lauren stood, keenly staring at the water, and then took her own little leap of faith as she dived into the sea and floated happily towards me as I sat in the back of our two-man receptacle. Once lifted in, she kept scooting around José who was in the front and would then proceed to dive in again. She loved it!

Ralph as it transpired, is more like his José in the water—a terrible swimmer! Following Lauren, he dived into the sea, came up spluttering and kicking his little legs madly and sending water flying everywhere. I reached for his squirmy little body and dragged him back onto my knee, where he stayed for the rest of the trip, shivering and making me feel incredibly guilty.

Now almost one, he still charges into the water and still has a look of shock on his face when he gets wet! Both he and Lauren are now much too big to sit comfortably on my lap but it hasn't stopped them trying.

After about six months of living together, José's project finished and we had to leave Mexico. It was much sooner than either of us anticipated and we didn't have much time to prepare and organise what we would do with the dogs. Luckily, on my travels I met some amazing people and one such couple was Kim and Terry. I met them at the Loral Langemeier event in San Diego during my first week of travels and when they found out the dogs needed to spend six months in the US before being allowed into Australia, Kim offered to help.

After only meeting her occasionally during my trip, it amazes me that she would offer to sacrifice her time and family life to look after my two dogs. This is no easy feat as Kim has two children, Kat and Max, and two young dogs of her own. On top of that she and Terry are holding down jobs and renovating houses too.

Like the majority of adults in the world, I watch terrible things on the news on a daily basis and admit over the years I had become jaded and cynical about the goodness of people... until this trip.

During the last year, time and again I have been witness to, and personally benefited from, the kindness of strangers. It has been a wonderful affirming experience and only strengthened my desire to help and serve others too.

Alaska
Date #53: José – My Last Official Date
When we left Mexico I wanted to show José some of America, the country I had fallen in love with as I travelled around and experienced all of its diversity from the amazing people to the different terrain, climate, sights and sounds.

And I wanted José to join me on my trip to my final US state—Alaska! Which is why he officially became my final date in the final state as he joined me on a cruise.

In spite of the cold weather, José and I enjoyed the trip immensely. When we stepped ahore in Juneau we headed off for a walk to the Mendenhall glacier, the ice field looking more like blue spiky frosted icing layered between the snow-capped mountains than the ice we are used to in European winters. It was José's first time seeing a glacier and the look on his face as he took it in made me feel warm inside despite the cold.

After braving the freezing temperatures we rewarded ourselves with a stiff drink in the Red Dog Saloon before heading back to the cruise ship and our onward destinations—Skagway and Ketchikan as well as Glacier Bay National Park.

The cruise was fantastic and despite me getting whooping cough and pneumonia, José—with his humorous antics—kept me laughing (and coughing!) and in good spirits for the whole trip.

During our travels to Alaska, around California and through a few other places in America, José and I kept hearing the Gotye song, *Somebody That I Used To Know.* No surprises then that it has been added to my US playlist to remind me of the terrific experience of being in the US with José.

CHAPTER 9

Evaluation...

The Final Stage of the Positive Change Formula

W hen I finished my trip I trained to become a coach. The coach training was an amazing ending to my journey and helped me synthesise and really integrate all the lessons I had learnt along the way into my daily actions.

When the training finished, I finally felt ready to sit down and have the hard conversations I needed with my parents, the ones I had shied away from on my first visit. I wanted to reconnect with my family.

I sat down separately with my mum and dad to finally share who I am, what I've been through and how it has shaped me. I'd hoped that if they understood me and my life a little better we could reconnect at a deeper level.

Although I knew my parents were proud of what I had achieved in my career, I felt they were always disappointed in my personal life. I had been brought up to be career-focussed and independent, however, what was expected of me had changed when I'd got older—and I hadn´t.

My dad, especially, seemed to attribute my lack of interest in cooking, general domesticity and bowing to the will of a male as the reason for my inability to maintain a relationship. He had advised me over the last few years that I needed to grow up, stop being so selfish and settle down. I hope that now he understands a little bit more why I have had difficulty in maintaining relationships and that it was actually bowing to the dominating will of a male when I was sixteen that had decimated my ability to have a loving, long-lasting relationship and had nothing to do with me being unable to cook.

Life after 50 Dates

It is now eighteen months after I started this crazy, life-affirming journey and I am finally back in Australia and excited at the prospect of starting a new adventure.

I know the question on all of your lips will be, 'Am I still with José?'

And whilst I would love to give you the fairy-tale Hollywood ending, I'm afraid I have to give you the real life version. No, I'm not.

After travelling around the US and Europe, José and I returned to his home country of Spain. He was still going through a drawn out and ugly divorce and was missing his daughter, which is very understandable.

Although I offered to stay in Spain and tried to be there to support José in his difficult time, the language barrier was proving more and more difficult as he got frustrated time and again that he could not talk to me fluently in Spanish about what he was going through in a way that I would understand immediately.

His frustration led to him keeping his feelings to himself and growing more and more distant from me. He was spiralling downwards, clearly feeling out of control in relation to his daughter and the divorce and, naturally, feeling guilty for hurting me as I bore the brunt of his anger.

I understood why he was acting as he was but it didn't stop it hurting. Despite my unwavering support and empathy, it simply wasn't enough.

At the same time the dogs in the US had developed bad hip and elbow dysplasia and both needed several operations, including stem cell surgery—all of which was going to be extremely expensive.

José didn't have the money to pay for it and seemed inclined to do the easy thing and put them down. Having saved them once however, I was not going to abandon them now. We had taken them on and even if José was willing to give up on them (and possibly me too), I was not.

And so, we agreed that I would return to Australia to save up some more cash, sort the dogs out and set up a home. José had said that despite all of the issues we were facing, he still loved me and wanted to be with me. He had been offered a job in Australia with one of his old work colleagues and assured me he would come over as soon as his divorce was finished and he had his head together.

Believing that the best thing for him, me and the dogs in the US was for me to leave and give him the time and space he required, I reluctantly said goodbye. As he walked away I noticed he never looked back and, although only moments before he had kissed me and told me we would be together again soon, I had a strong feeling that I would never see him again.

However, I accepted what he said in good faith and despite his recent actions had no reason not to believe him. But my intuition was correct. After I left the country he became more and more distant as he demonstrated he no longer cared whether he hurt me or not.

I've found that humans do what animals do when they feel cornered, desperate and uncertain—they attack. Many people become unkind and spiteful when faced with having to make tough choices and decisions, José was one of them.

Was I upset by his behaviour? Obviously, yes. I am human with all the feelings and emotions that go along with that.

Am I broken by his betrayal of my trust? No. Do I think what happened is my fault? No. Obviously I've considered my actions throughout the relationship with a view to lessons learnt and what I can do better next time but I know in this case I did all I could to make the relationship work.

I am not able to control, nor am I responsible for, the actions of others, only my own. I did nothing except the right thing by José. I can go to bed at night with a clear conscience and look myself in the mirror and be happy with what I see.

Am I going to give up on finding a partner who is an honest, loyal and loving man? Hell, no! Am I going to drop my standards and settle for second best? Dream on sunshine!

Do I think that this one event means that my Positive Change Formula doesn't work—no way!

I have come so far as a result of this journey. I have let go of my grief. I have found a new passion for coaching. I believe in myself again. I believe in the beauty of the universe and the kindness of strangers. I have a renewed interest in life and living. And I finally know my purpose.

So, honestly, I can hand on heart say that the formula works. Plus, I now have three incredibly wonderful dogs who will always love me no matter what. I feel very blessed and importantly, I have no regrets.

CHAPTER 10

The Positive Change Formula in Action All Over Again

When I got back to Australia in January 2013, I took the time to reflect and examine my own life as it stands now, which is the final step in the formula. I pulled out the laminated list of goals from my wallet and re-read my initial set of ambitions.

- Find a partner;
- Reconnect with my family and society in general;
- Spend time with my friends and have weekends off to relax;
- Regain my health and fitness;
- Change jobs to a career that feeds all of my intellectual parts, including my mind, body and spirit;
- Relocate to the countryside where I feel most at peace;
- Travel... a lot; and
- Break out of my routine, have some fun and adventures again.

Looking at the list, almost all of my goals have been achieved.

Happily, I'm now reconnected with my family and friends and value the time with them, even if it is only via Skype.

I've certainly travelled and broken out of my comfort zone. In fact, I ran away from it like a crazy woman with arms flailing wildly!

Although I still love the law and government relations, I want to do that *and* coach others to achieve their own positive changes. We all benefit from knowing our purpose and more so from actually living it. There is something about doing what we love and what comes naturally that makes our whole world seem so much better.

And finally, in seeking more balance in life, I have been prioritising my health over work. When we care for and nurture ourselves—body, mind and spirit—we seem to find a greater sense of calm and understanding around where we want to be, live and what we want to do with the rest of our lives.

Whilst chatting to Rachael about my new situation whilst walking up Mt Taylor as we used to before I left (some things don't change!) I had an 'A-ha' moment. We don't need a soul mate to stand beside us to be happy, we need to be happy within our own souls—effectively we are our own soul mates!

Now reconnected with me and trusting in myself again, I love who I am and I am proud of who I am, how I treat others and what I have achieved—not just as a result of this journey but throughout my life. I wish we could all feel that sense of fulfilment and contentment in life. We certainly all deserve to.

Looking back at the feelings of self-loathing that I was experiencing before my trip it is amazing to me that I feel so different now—even though I am single again and back where I started from a geographic perspective.

Maybe we all need to let go of the past in order to successfully grow and move forward. Whether that is through letting go of grief, trusting yourself again, letting go of some past hurt and anger or simply forgiving yourself for your mistakes. It seems that we grow mostly by learning more, accepting more, and being kinder towards ourselves than through any external source.

We don't need a partner in life to be happy. We need to be happy and love ourselves first—because after all we live in our own bodies and minds for our entire life, no-one else does!

And again, the universe seemed to confirm this for me in a quote I read the other day in a magazine article. 'Are you still looking for that one special person who can positively change your life?' it asked. And then went on to say '...Then take a look in the mirror and you will find them.'

The message really resonated. I didn't need to go around the US, I didn't need to find the man of my dreams. I could probably have stayed right here in Australia where I started and it would have made no difference because all I really needed to do was get to know and love me again!

That said, I've learnt a valuable lesson through Adam's death, this trip and my relationships with Sam and José—more than ever it is apparent that despite our fervent wishes to the contrary, we cannot control the future nor other people or their emotions. However, we can control ourselves, our own mind, our thoughts, our feelings.

Remembering the pain and regret of not telling Adam I loved him when I could, I know now that whatever anyone else does, I need to be true to myself. Whether it makes me vulnerable or not, I need to share my true feelings with those I love.

And as long as we remain true to ourselves and our hearts, we can have no regrets. There is more strength in allowing ourselves to be vulnerable than weakness.

Kick-Start the Positive

So, given I've completed almost all of my original goals, I settled down to write some new ones, applying my Positive Change Formula to my new circumstances. Starting again with **P for Problems,** which is where we really look at what we are experiencing, why and how it's affecting us, I tore out some clean sheets of paper and started to mind-map.

Looking at all areas of my life it is no surprise that there was a huge difference between where I am now to where I was before my trip. Yes, I have some problem areas still and no doubt always will, but these are far fewer and less drastic than before.

In relation to family and friends, having fun and being social, health, spiritual and emotional wellbeing, and physical environment all of those things are in pretty good shape.

However, I do now need to work on my finances, career and, yes, romance is back on the list.

Now conscious of my past workaholic tendencies, burying my feelings, not looking after myself, focusing too much on money and my career rather than what enriches my soul, I wanted to be mindful of all of those as I worked through my options. So I wrote them down and stuck them to my computer on post-it notes to remind me of them.

Then I let my brain flit from one idea to the next as I settled down and brainstormed my options.

Maybe it wasn't surprising that in looking at any future work or career my heart was in complete contrast with my head.

My head told me to get as much money as I could as quickly as possible by returning to a lobbyist role like the one I had before— effectively selling my soul again to a corporate entity.

But my heart sank at this prospect. It wanted me to pursue the purpose I had finally found in my life, which was to help other people make their own positive changes through coaching.

Looking at my current financial situation it was evident that whilst what my heart wants is a lovely idea, the harsh reality is running a company as my sole source of income is not an option—I need money for rent, bills, food, and most importantly, dogs operations.

However, as always, spending time to mind-map options always provides other more creative solutions.

In relation to finding a partner again, I realised that at this point I want to put it on the back-burner. It may sound selfish but I want to pursue my own happiness right now. Plus, realistically I need to give myself time to get over José. I don't want to rush back out there charging around like the proverbial bull in a China shop and not learning the lessons I am meant to.

This time I am having a break (but not for six years). And, when I am ready, I will get back out there and resume my search.

Dating over fifty men across the US has had its benefits in that I now have a super clear idea of what I do and don't want in a partner. All of those attributes are listed safely in a special notepad and will be kept safe for future reference.

Having worked out the path I wanted to take in relation to my work, finances and love life, I had a nagging feeling that there was something missing but I couldn't quite work out what.

After a couple of days I still didn't have an answer. So, I did something my dad had taught me years ago when career and future planning—I wrote my eulogy.

Strange how thinking about our own death and how we want to be remembered focuses our minds on the present and what is important, which can result in sudden clarity.

For me, this is when my mind confirmed one ambition and provided me with a completely new one.

I added my two new goals to the list and added a few other intentions which sprang to mind. And this is why my list of goals now contains the following:

- Find work in Canberra that provides me with a decent living but that doesn't take up every waking minute of every day so I can also spend time walking Jess and hanging out with my friends.
- Set up my own business: *Positive Change Coaching and Consulting* and work weekends and evenings to become the best coach I can to help others fulfil their dreams.
- Once my business is doing well move it, me and Jessie to America where I can join the other dogs Ralph and Lauren. And, importantly, so I can pay it forward to the country and people who have given me so much as I travelled through.
- Make enough money to build a school for girls who live in rural Nepal and sponsor as many as I can each year until fulfilling this ambition.

- Remember the good times with all those people who have been important to me throughout my life and be true to myself and my feelings so that I have no regrets in the future.
- Be kind to myself, even when a 'Mel moment' happens and I humiliate myself, as I no doubt will at many points!
- Understand that everything is temporary so make the most out of each day for even the darkest days will pass.
- Continue my quest for a partner and don't ever settle for second best.
- Remain true to myself and trust in my head, heart and very importantly my little voice.
- Try to be the person in life that JFK referred to when he said, 'One person can make a difference and everyone should try.'

And finally:

- Enjoy the journey!

I have no doubt during the upcoming implementation phase more issues will arise to challenge me, but, as before, with tenacity and integrity, I will keep ploughing forward sure in the end that victory will be mine. And this time what a sweet victory it will be as I help others too rather than just me.

I can literally close my eyes and see, hear and feel the people who will benefit from finally taking the steps to reaching their own goals, make their own positive changes and living their true purpose.

And I can clearly see the faces and hear the chattering excited voices of the little girls in Nepal as they happily play outside the new school I plan to build them.

Those images will sustain me through whatever obstacles are thrown into my path and, with my new list safely in my wallet, I have a tangible daily reminder too.

If there is one thing I have learnt during this last eighteen months that I want to share with you it is this: it isn't selfish to live the life you choose and to follow your dreams.

Whether you are a man, woman, a girl or a boy, this is your life and you only get one shot. It isn't a rehearsal so don't waste it by hiding your true nature to accommodate the wishes of others.

If you want to make positive changes in your own life, you don't have to sell up and travel across America, you don't even need to go looking for love. That was my journey and everyone has their own.

Yours may be making small changes that provide you with more time with your family, more harmony at work, more peace in your life or more balance. Or it may be that you prioritise looking for love too.

There is no right or wrong to living the Positive Change Formula, it is a structure and formula to help identify, create and implement the changes you want in your life, but there is room to improvise. You just need to be clear of your issues, what you want to change and fulfil the steps needed to implement those changes that are right for you... in the time that is right for you.

Just don't give up! Despite breaks or distractions. Despite the hardships, twists and turns in the roads, or having to go back and start again. Don't stop!

If it is important to you, keep making steps towards your goal and you will achieve it in the end. And if you need assistance—ask for it!

Find someone you admire and trust, whether it is a friend, family member or coach. Find someone to hold you accountable and keep you moving forward... Believe me, it's worth it.

As the Chinese proverb says, 'Jump... and the net will find you!'

Epilogue

I wrote to Adam this morning as I still do often. It was my final letter to him before finishing this book.

Darling Adamski,

Well, here I am! I know today I will finally finish writing the story that it seems I was destined to tell.

It's now been over eighteen months since I left Australia and I am back home again with a new set of audacious goals to fulfil.

This journey has been one hell of an adventure and I have felt you with me at many stages along the way. I know that, just as you have over the last eighteen months, you will again watch over me and support me from afar in achieving my new ambitions.

I have no doubt you are proud of me and happy for me. You were an amazing and special man.

I still think of you every day but now I remind myself of how lucky I am to have had you in my life for all of those years. Eighteen years of friendship, Adam, it's a beautiful thing.

I am so grateful that I took the leap of faith and had some time to rediscover and chase my dreams. Amazingly, in seeking a new soul mate I realised two things. The first, my darling Adam, is that you are and always will be my soul mate whether you are with me physically or spiritually.

The second is that I am also my own soul mate. In understanding and loving myself I have found so much more contentment that I ever did when relying on someone else to provide me with my source of happiness.

My inner voice is here with me stronger than ever and holding me accountable. Everything I need to survive is within me and now I know that I am not scared—no matter what twists and turns life takes.

I am ready to move forward, Adamski, and at some point along this journey, I have finally accepted that you are not coming back.

I will always miss you and although I don't know how much time I have left before I see you again, please know that you will always be my soul mate and never be forgotten.

Sweet dreams Adamski—until we meet again x

Afterword

During my time in the UK in June 2012, my Aunty Barb got very sick and was rushed to hospital.

Although I had missed being with Adam at his bedside when he was sick, I was granted the privilege of being with her for her last few days.

I was with my cousin, Deb, in the early hours when Aunty Barb passed away and although the memories are painful, I would not have had it any other way.

It seems like no coincidence to me that she died on the same day Adam had passed four years earlier—23rd of June.

Aunty Barb knew I was writing this book and was—as always—fully supportive and encouraging of what I was doing.

Whilst she was in hospital I made her two promises. Finishing this was one of them.

I promised you I'd do it m'duck. Good night. God bless x

About the Author

Melanie Brocklehurst was born in Cambridge, England. She was lucky enough to travel and live abroad while growing up, which created an insatiable wanderlust that has taken her around the world.

Melanie started her career as an environmental lawyer in England, however, her adventures took her to Australia where she settled, and, has at various times been an Officer in the Australian Army Legal Corps, Legal Adviser to Ministers and a political lobbyist for a global international company.

From there, she decided to implement her Positive Change Formula for a year, and set off on a new adventure taking her to every state in the US... and to Mexico!

As a result of her trip she set up her own business, *Positive Change Coaching and Consulting*, and—with a little help from computer technology—

is coaching people around the world on how to make their own positive life changes.

If you would like to read about what Melanie is up to now and what is happening with her new goals, please feel free to follow her blog at www.50datesin50statesbook.com.

If you want to find out more about Melanie's coaching, go to www.positive-change-coaching.com

or email Melanie about her one-on-one coaching and programs at: info@positive-change-coaching.com

Positive Change Coaching And Consulting

With over 15 years of experience working as a lawyer, ministerial adviser and political lobbyist, Melanie Brocklehurst decided it was time for a change—a positive change.

In her memoir, *50 Dates in 50 States: One Woman's Journey to Positive Change* Melanie shares with you her formula for achieving positive results, looking not only at what you **want** to change but **why** and **how**.

Having become an executive and life coach, speaker, and author, Melanie, driven to help others achieve their own success, founded *Positive Change Coaching and Consulting*—a coaching and seminar business. Through her business Melanie coaches individuals and provides seminars on her 8-Step *Positive Change* Program to people who want to achieve success and positive results in their own lives.

Combining her Positive Change Formula with traditional coaching and neuro-linguistic programming techniques, Melanie is helping people all over the world both as a coach and speaker by providing people with the tools they need to create the specific positive changes they want.

If you want to find out more about Melanie's coaching, go to www.positive-change-coaching.com

or email Melanie about her one-on-one coaching and programs at: info@positive-change-coaching.com

For media queries please contact: media@positive-change-coaching.com

Acknowledgements

Special thanks go to:

- Ann Brocklehurst (mum) for all of your love, support and encouragement in this process. Love you x
- David Brocklehurst (dad) for your sage advice over the years, accepting my sudden life changes with grace and loving me despite not understanding some of my choices. Love you x
- Aunty Barb (Barbara Middleton) for your love and support throughout my life. I owe you one final promise and I intend to keep it.
- Deborah Bargh for always being there for me to turn to – you are my rock. Dubs ya x
- Ghis and Phil Kearon who saved my life when I was 16 and have felt responsible for it ever since. Thank you for being my surrogate parents for the past 20 years. Love you x
- Daisy, Andrew and Kiara Wilson for being my Aussie family and for looking after both me and Jessie when we needed it. Love you x

- Margaret and David Hays for allowing me to write about your son, Adam.
- Isabel Ault for helping me survive university.
- Annie Kwan for Nepal and always being an inspiration.
- Jo Bransby for showing me there is more to life than work, leaving corporate life before me to become one of the best personal trainers in Melbourne.
- Georgia Ramsay for always being up for a bacon and egg roll.
- Rachael Jackson for being Thelma to my Louise—*Dennys!*
- Loral Langemeier for suggesting I write this in the first place and creating a situation which gave me no other choice than to do so.

To the people without whom I could not have made this journey, I would like to thank:

- Kim Bozell, Terry Kloepfer, Kat and Max Thomson for welcoming my dogs, Ralph and Lauren into your family. Thanks for being my American sister, Kim, couldn't ask for a better one!
- Nathan Winn for looking after the majority of my worldly goods
- Kim Williams and her mum, Jill, for looking after the rest and making the room even when baby Caitlin Jean arrived!
- Lorence Eshoe for providing me with a safe haven in the US.
- Larry Michaels at Match Matrix for allowing me free use of your services in an attempt to see if my potential dates were worth it!
- Renee Furbush of Off Centre Skin Care, Hartford, CT.
- Jessica Lorentz at Epic Bodyworks Massage, Minneapolis.

To the people who helped me in the process of writing this book, I would like to thank:

- Cynthia Lamb for being such a wonderful editor and now friend.
- John C. Robinson for being a great book coach and helping me through the rough patches.
- Bonnie Boezeman AO, Marla Martensen and Charmaine Hammond for your amazing support and encouragement.

- Lucian James, Jo Bransby, Andrew Machon, Annie Kwan, Kim Bozell, Rachael Jackson and Daisy Wilson for providing feedback along the way

And I also want to thank the following people for being part of my life and my journey.

Family: Ann Brocklehurst & Ian Hill-Pickford; David & Janet Brocklehurst; Nicola and my fabulous niece and nephew, Daniel and Lucy Wade; Barbara, Keith, David, Caren, Cara and Cian Middleton; Debbie, David, Sam, Nathan and Jacob Bargh; Malcolm, Luke, Josh, Jordan, Bethany and Joel Brocklehurst; Melvyn and Pam Brocklehurst; Wendy Morford; Dave and Doreen Blockley; Michelle, Steve, Liam and Jake Symonds; Geraldine, Georgina and Jamie Naughton; Stephen, Rachael, Christine, Stephen Cadywould and Anna McCarthy.

UK: Isabel Ault, Caroline May, Sarah Middleton, Karen Hyland, James Goldsbrough, Lucy Wheatcroft, Andrea Milward, Jean Snoxell, Lindsey Adderson, Alison Ibbotson and Georgie Browne.

Australia: Kevin and Barb Rowe, Tony, Carolyn, Chris, Andrew and Sarah Howe, Yvette Kerr, Rachael Jackson and Simon Kelly, Jacinda Hoskins, Victoria Prowse, Aleksandra James, Vera Krisko-Jowe, Isla Hale, Mark Brady, Peter Hammond, Nicole Macdonald, Graeme, Judy and Emma Howard, Kathryn Jones, Elisabeth Bateson, Anne Kinsella, Beth Parkin, Belinda Dennett, Nicolette Maury-Vassy, Naomi Viccars and Damien Coke, Greer Harris, Narelle Morley and Claire Burleigh, Scott Marett and Christine Cartledge.

US: Katrina Johnson and Joel Toney, Renata Dionello, Richard Nash, Stefan Krawczyk, Greg Carver, Julie Walker, Barry Murphy.

The Live out Loud community: Tracy Blay, Dona Donato, Nancy Sherman, Ellie Josephs and Joyce Gass, Annette Magee, Shannon Gutierrez, Sarita Stevens, Jana and Ricky Colter, Elizabeth Pitt, Randy Tate and Karen Baur, Eric Metcalf, Valerie Soeters, Rebekah Hall, Ken Course, Mike Mullen, Jennifer Walsh Jedow, Larry Micheal, Jiah Miesel, Hope Suhr as well as many other wonderful supportive people.

My friends from the Academy of Coaching and NLP: Andrew Machon, Diana Harris, Lindsay Hahn McDonnell, Linda Marchesani, Mindy Kobara-Mates, Lucian James, Terri Sullivant, Laurie Cozart, Elena Nagorskaya, Audrey Green, Elaine Alves De Jesus, Ilona Ivannikova, Ivar Lukk, Kim Von Berg, Cheryl McCormick, Tara Lee Ford, Mumtaz Levent Akkol, Ed Martin, Maggie Kilbourne, Karen Feltes, Fiona Wong, Matt Cusick, Jannick Pitot Rosenblatt, Simone Janssen, Jaime Gonzalez Molins, Hong Xu, Linda Delgado, Benita Jacque, Rossana Magana Ruiz, Tim Callan. And last but certainly not least to a wonderful trainer and coach, Helen Attridge – I will try and make you proud!

Singapore: Rich Atkinson, Steven Liew and Simon Flann.

Mexico: Juli Goff at Se Habla... La Paz for teaching me Spanish and allowing me to speak in words rather than simply gestures!

France: Julie and Charlie Elston for your lasting friendship and support x